It's Our Country

Indigenous Arguments For Meaningful Constitutional Recognition And Reform

Edited By Megan Davis
Marcia Langton

16
EasyRead Large

RHYW

Copyright Page from the Original Book

MELBOURNE UNIVERSITY PRESS
An imprint of Melbourne University Publishing Limited
11–15 Argyle Place South, Carlton, Victoria 3053, Australia
mup-info@unimelb.edu.au
www.mup.com.au

First published 2016

Cover design by Design by Committee
Typeset by Sonya Murphy, Typeskill
Printed in Australia by McPherson's Printing Group

National Library of Australia Cataloguing-in-Publication entry

It's our country: Indigenous arguments for meaningful constitutional recognition and reform/editors: Megan Davis, Marcia Langton.

9780522869934 (paperback)
9780522869941 (ebook)

Subjects: Aboriginal Australians—Legal status, laws, etc.
Aboriginal Australians—Government relations.
Aboriginal Australians—Civil rights.
Constitutional law—Australia.

Davis, Megan, 1975– editor.
Langton, Marcia, 1951– editor.

323.119915

TABLE OF CONTENTS

We dedicate this book to Faith Bandler and the 1967 campaigners.

We acknowledge that we owe a debt to the courageous men and women who pursued constitutional change for more than a decade in the 1950s and 1960s and dedicate this book to them. Their hard work, funded by private donations, often from Aboriginal and Torres Strait Islander senior people contributing from their pensions, resulted in the only referendum in Australian history dealing with issues pertaining to fundamental fairness and justice for Indigenous Australians.

The great hope of many Australians is that we can achieve a second referendum asking Australians to vote for recognising us as first Australians in the Constitution. If we should achieve this most important goal, we trust that Australians will pause to consider those brave souls who succeeded against all odds in persuading the Australian Government to hold the first referendum on our status in 1967.

FOREWORD

Fred Chaney

This book presents a window into the challenge facing those trying to advance constitutional recognition of the native peoples of Australia and exposes the potential underlying fault line between black and white thinking on constitutional recognition. Bridging that fault line is essential to success. Can the wider community bring itself to understand and embrace the perspectives of the first nation peoples on their place and circumstances?

The seventeen contributors, all Aboriginal and/or Torres Strait Islander people, put forward their varying perspectives on the importance and value of constitutional change. The differences between them relate to means and not ends. In their different ways, they all talk about their collective identities, their survival, their ongoing rights as collectives or first nations. They want recognition to make a difference or the adoption of alternative approaches, treaties, representation or legislation. They want recognition of continuing difference as well as greater statistical equality. Closing the gap is not enough. Their aim is not assimilation and disappearance. Their aim is to end the anxiety about the continuing existence of their cultures.

We commonly claim that one of the distinctive elements of Australia is that it is the home of the world's oldest living cultures. The claim is true. The implications of that claim are profound and not widely understood. It means that the cultures are not historic; they are alive in Australia today. If history is any guide, they will live in Australia in the future because Aboriginal people will ensure that they do. This is a choke point for many other Australians: we are all equal and the same, aren't we?

Recognition is about continuing difference. As these essays make clear, Aboriginal and Torres Strait Islander peoples form part of the rich tapestry of our country and the reality of their ongoing existence is recognised in domestic law. Year after year, parts of the Tindale map of the tribes of Australia are converted into areas legally recognised as places where collective rights exist in the tribes who were here before the rest of us. These rights flow from the tribal or collective status of the peoples who were here when the settlers arrived.

Regularly agreements are struck between miners and native titleholders on whose land they work. These are not agreements between mining companies and individual Aboriginal people. The agreements are between those companies and the Aboriginal collectives whose country it is.

In Western Australia, historically a place of fierce opposition to Aboriginal land rights, the state government has treatied about the South West lands not with 37,000 individual Noongars but with their collective identities defined by their own law and culture. Post Mabo, it is unremarkable that Aboriginal people are dealt with as people identified through connection to country. For some purposes at least, first nation identity has been established and recognised in the law.

Indigenous Australians won a great victory in Mabo: recognition of their unique continuing status within the Australian polity. For constitutional recognition to mean anything to them, it must be an advance on what they have already achieved after centuries of non-recognition. At the minimum, it must cement in gains already made.

What all of these writers provide are measures against which proposals for constitutional change can be measured. Are there better alternatives?

What they also provide is a window into the perspective of native people on their circumstances and their deep sense of powerlessness and injustice. They tell us why change is wanted. As an older white Australian faced with the reality of continuing disadvantage, I sometimes console myself with their victories over fifty years: voting rights achieved, full and equal citizenship, land rights, the Racial Discrimination Act, the Mabo decision, cultural excellence, and expanded agreement-making. But how can anyone deny their dissatisfaction—even rage—at their circumstances and powerlessness in the face of often counter-productive government interventions in their lives? Every problem is to be solved by reducing their individual agency rather than enlisting individual and collective agency.

Recent years have seen a steady destruction of the organisations through which Aboriginal people found their voices and the chance to participate in designing and delivering solutions. It is suggested these are the worst of times to be considering recognition because Indigenous affairs are in such a sorry state. Their ideas about how to go about the business of closing the gaps are subservient to the superior knowledge of politicians and bureaucrats. Problems that can only be solved locally in homes, classes and workplaces are to be solved in manners dictated from a distant centre. Despite valiant efforts by Aboriginal leaders, policy and administration are more centralised than ever before.

So the essays ask many questions and pose a variety of answers. They point out the interrelatedness of proposals for constitutional recognition with policy and legislation. They provide some tests to apply to any proposal the parliament might put forward for consideration in a referendum. Is the proposal one that confirms the ongoing place of our first nations in the Australian legal and political system? Does it in any way threaten or diminish what has already been gained through the past struggles for recognition of rights and status? Does it provide a framework within which our first nation peoples may continue to assert their identities and pursue agreements with governments and corporations to deal with the issues raised in these essays, including continuing disadvantage? If a proposal fails these tests, it is unlikely to command the support of those we are wishing to recognise and would not command mine.

Pursuing agreements that acknowledge Aboriginal identities as tribes or first nations and which deal with the issues they wish to have addressed is an attractive option. They are not subject to the tyranny of a referendum and the danger posed by the double majority requirement. First nations come to the table as stakeholders, not as supplicants. They can determine what they wish to negotiate. They do not have to be limited by the legal complexities of native title law. As the Yorta Yorta proclaimed after the High Court denied their native title claim: we are here and you have to deal with us. Assertion of first nation state is a political action rather than a necessarily circumscribed legal claim.

INTRODUCTION

Megan Davis and Marcia Langton

Aboriginal peoples are the first peoples of this continent by an immeasurably long period of time—currently it is believed we go back at least 60,000 years. As a result of that long occupancy and ownership of this continent, we have a distinct cultural identity and traditions and practices, including a unique connection to sea and country that ought to be recognised and retained as part of our nation's social fabric.

To ally the fears of some of our readers, a note on our use of the term 'country' in the title of this collection is necessary. In most Indigenous cultures in Australia, land is regarded not just as a physical resource, but as a social resource: 'country' is the term used by many Indigenous people to refer to customary estates. These landscapes are defined and bound by custom and hereditary rights, shaped by *a priori* spiritual forces and imbued with spiritual power. 'Country' may include landscapes, seascapes and riverscapes, and may have one or more focal sacred sites. These sites may be terrestrial, marine or riparian. The use of the term 'country' permits a more careful account of Indigenous cultural and social concerns and aspirations and opens up the possibility of analysing the use of 'country' in terms relevant to the Indigenous stewards. 'Country' may include land and water, whether owned under Australian title or not, and in the latter case, whether or not under claim under native title or other legislation, or land and water under contemporary forms of Indigenous governance, including local customary forms of governance, representative bodies, community councils, etc. Customary management of 'country' involves special knowledge and practices that the traditional owners bring to the task.

Over the years since Australia's Federation there have been calls by many Australians for the recognition of that unique cultural status as first peoples as well as the right to be treated equally. We achieved this in part in 1967 when a majority of Australians voted to amend the Constitution to recognise Aboriginal and Torres Strait Islander peoples as a part of the Australian nation. In the near future Australians will be called upon again to collaborate with Aboriginal and Torres Strait Islander peoples in the next phase in constitutional recognition.

The Australian people will be asked to participate in a conversation about those two things: how should first peoples be recognised in the fabric of our nation and should we commit to equality of all peoples? These are deceptively simple questions for a number of reasons. The Australian Constitution is not easily amended. Constitutional change is fraught with difficult legal questions relating to the potential for future court activism, interpretation and many other issues.

Yet consistent polling from the past five years has shown that most Australians agree that we must secure a path to honouring the status and culture of Indigenous peoples, as well as committing to equality before the law. There are many points of view on how we might achieve that. This is one of the purposes of this collection of essays authored by Aboriginal and Torres Strait Islander people: to publish the diverse and often surprising views and approaches of a range of Indigenous public intellectuals and community leaders. We asked authors not to be constrained by the ideological minefield of deeply held views from both the left and right wings of Australian political life regarding matters such as 'rights' in the Constitution. If societies were to confine themselves only to what the most conservative and tradition-bound will abide, there would be no change and no law reform.

Still, we acknowledge and respect the deep commitment of some to a rights-free polity. The strength of the sentiment among a few against rights does make the job of overcoming the Commonwealth's power to discriminate racially, which it has had since 1901, our most difficult challenge. How do we find a way to resolve the problem of the racially discriminatory nature of our Constitution apropos the opposition to explicit rights? The answer may be that we as a nation cease to identify Indigenous peoples as a 'race' but rather as 'first peoples and the descendants of first peoples'. We are confident most

Australians do not want our Indigenous cultures, our languages and all those distinctive things that pre-date British annexation to disappear, or to contribute in any way to the disappearance or demise of Aboriginal and Torres Strait Islander peoples and cultures. Dilemmas such as these present us all, as collaborators on the recognition project, with most interesting challenges.

When we talk about the recognition of Aboriginal and Torres Strait Islander peoples, what do we mean? More precisely, what do we mean by the term 'recognition'? This collection of essays developed from a concern that the public conversation on recognition had become too constrained. The word recognition infers an acknowledgement of someone or something, a fairly innocuous endeavour—simple and uncontroversial. However, in the field of law and politics, recognition is complex, especially Indigenous recognition. Recognition lies on a spectrum of reform that extends from acknowledgement through to concrete and substantive rights. The words recognition and recognise, in the absence of an open and transparent debate about proposals, were constraining the public conversation to a mistaken presupposition that Indigenous recognition is and always has been about symbolism. This is not the case. The campaign for recognition over the years has always been expressed as a *package* of measures that includes symbols, legal and political reform, and rights.

Symbols are important. No one knows that better than the first peoples. Our culture and our rituals are filled with symbols. Our distinctive flag, for example, the red, black and yellow, is a symbol of our struggle for rights, our pride and solidarity: our blood, our skin and the land. Yet a symbol can also have a negative impact. It can have a detrimental effect if you are using it because it is low cost and risk free and because it ignores what it is people are trying to say. And what have the first peoples been trying to say?

Over the years there have been many attempts by Indigenous people to communicate to the Australian people the kind of recognition they seek. David Unaipon called for increased Indigenous autonomy and representation in 1926. Fred Maynard called for equality and equal citizenship rights and for the control of Indigenous affairs in 1927. Joe Anderson, the great King Burraga, chief of the Thurawal tribe in 1933, urged the prime minister to collaborate with Aboriginal people to give us a voice: 'All the black man wants is representation in federal parliament. There is also plenty of fish in the river for us all, and land to grow all we want.' William Cooper petitioned King George V for Indigenous representation in parliament in 1937. Doug Nicholls wrote to Ben Chifley in 1949 calling for Indigenous representation in federal parliament. In 1963, the Yirrkala bark petitions called for the government to talk to Yolngu people before making decisions about their land and their lives. Galarrwuy Yunupingu presented the Barunga Statement to Prime

Minister Hawke in 1988, the Bicentenary year, on behalf of the leaders of the clans and tribes of Northern and Central Australia. They called for a treaty to recognise Indigenous peoples and their rights to self-determination and self-management. Hawke promised and never delivered. In 2008, after the Apology to the Stolen Generations, the Yolngu again petitioned the Commonwealth through their senior Dilak, led again by Galarrwuy Yunupingu, asking Prime Minister Kevin Rudd to constitutionally recognise Indigenous rights. That same year, in a famous speech at Melbourne University, Galarrwuy reminded us that constitutional recognition was 'serious business' and about 'serious constitutional reform'. The submissions to the Expert Panel on Constitutional Recognition of Aboriginal and Torres Strait Islander Peoples in 2011 and to the Joint Select Committee in 2015 saw thousands of Indigenous organisations and individuals express support for constitutional recognition of many things, including participation and self-determination.

The message over the years from Aboriginal people has always been a plea to adjust Australia's constitutional arrangements so that our people can take better control of our lives and own the responsibility for our children's futures. The kind of recognition first peoples seek is one of empowerment and making space for the first peoples to play an active role in the nation. This explains why the ambiguity of the word recognition has led to a dissonance between the campaign to recognise and the Aboriginal political domain. The government campaign funded by the taxpayer to prosecute a 'Yes' vote has no agreed model to spruik to the Australian public, so they have been spruiking a softer version of reform. This has animated a suspicion and anxiety in the Aboriginal and Torres Strait Islander community about what *form* recognition will take and has unwittingly inspired a resistance to recognise. The resistance is also because of the drift in the debate. There have been four processes in five years with no decisive response from the government. The leaders of all major parties have valiantly preserved multi-party support but the years are ticking over.

People often dismiss the length of time it is taking, 2011 to now, by referring to the 1967 Referendum, which took approximately ten years. However, a clear-eyed view of the 1967 Referendum campaign reveals some important distinctions that we must bear in mind. Back then there was an unambiguous goal: Commonwealth responsibility for Aboriginal and Torres Strait Islander affairs and an amendment/s more than ten years out from the referendum. In fact the first sign of change came within a decade of Federation: that Aboriginal affairs must become a national responsibility. The 1967 Referendum campaign did not divide Aboriginal Australia. It had universal support, it had consensus between Indigenous groups and non-Indigenous groups, and it took place against a backdrop of a rapidly changing Australia. The protection era was giving way to the assimilation era and the manifestations of compulsory racial segregation and its failures were visible to the naked eye. Today, five years into a process, there is no model and there is no consensus as yet. There is no useful comparison to be made to 1967 except that it involves the Constitution, a referendum and Indigenous peoples. The 1967 Referendum should be remembered on its own for a wonderful achievement of collaboration between Indigenous and non-Indigenous Australia.

The difference between 1967 and today should be celebrated: we have a small but growing middle class and a vibrant cultural industry, including performance and art and successful Indigenous business men and women. There has been much progress and much to be positive about. We are pleased that there is a referendum council to shepherd this process to its next phase. With this process, we stand at a crossroad. There are two paths from here. One is the path of listening and *not hearing.* And the other is the path of listening and *hearing.* Before we arrive at an agreed position we, as a nation, need to learn how to listen and *hear* what it is the first peoples are saying. Jill Stauffer, who has written about 'ethical loneliness' and the injustice of not being heard, describes this ethical loneliness as the 'failure of just-minded people to hear well—from those who have suffered—what recovery or reconciliation after massive violence or long-standing injustice would require'. [1] According to Stauffer, this failure to hear *haunts* the goal of political transition, reconciliation or forgiveness.

This challenge—for Australia to hear what it is that Aboriginal and Torres Strait Islander peoples are saying about what recovery and reconciliation means to them—lies at the heart of this collection of essays.

The ideas and concrete proposals for reform contained in this collection of essays are Indigenous ways of explaining to Australians how to remedy and address the 'multiple ethical lapses' of the settled state. Being honest about these lapses does not run counter to optimism or impede collaboration. It is a matter of fact that unaddressed harms do not disappear. Communities and individuals do not just 'get over' wrongs but rather they 'colour the affective relations between persons and communities, haunting the official sites of transition and reconciliation'. [2] If we as a nation are truly committed to moving forward, then constitutional recognition can be that vehicle if we commit to something we have not done before as a nation: listen and hear what Aboriginal and Torres Strait Islander peoples have to say about our democratic governance and how it may be improved.

It is clear from this collection of essays that such renovation and improvement of the way our democracy *hears* Indigenous peoples does not involve dramatic constitutional change but rather a series of staggered steps that involve policy, legislation and constitutional reform over a period of time. The language of a package approach or staggered approach has emerged because it is apparent in the sixth year of a lingering process that the Constitution is not enough. There are many other low-cost, low-risk, non-constitutional ideas that would receive support. For those of you reading this book, this may be the first time you have read about the long-held aspirations of the Aboriginal and Torres Strait Islander peoples. It is our wish that you hear what it is that successive governments have failed to hear and develop a better understanding of why many communities will not settle for the approaches that have already been tried and failed: symbolism, gradualism, minimalist approaches.

***

The book is not divided into themes. There was an unrehearsed symmetry to the chapters. We invited a broad range of first nations people to submit a chapter on constitutional recognition; their visions for reform. We did not restrain authors by the parameters of the current recognition project. We found a not unremarkable unanimity with authors linking policy, statute and constitutional amendment as equally important levers of reform. This provides political decision-makers with some guidance about what reform should not be limited to. We must be flexible. Because constitutional reform was on the agenda five years ago does not mean it has to be on the agenda now. Reform must suit the milieu and it must be sensible. It may be other reforms are more urgent and the steps are staggered. Perhaps big-C constitutional recognition (the amendments to its text) comes later.

In the current debate we are hearing two things. One is the suggestion Aboriginal and Torres Strait Islander peoples will not be able to come to a consensus. These essays show that there is a consensus. There is a consensus that 'weak' form recognition is not enough. This is being described in a number of ways by commentators as 'gradualism', 'minimalism' or 'incremental'. The consensus is broadly that the following is not enough: a few lines of acknowledgement, deletion of section 25 and moderation of the races power (section 51[xxvi]). The other message from these essays is the consensus on policy. The recognition council has been set work to do during the lowest ebb in Indigenous policy for decades. If the policy settings are not addressed in this process then the project will be hampered.

Noel Pearson writes about the deep, seething impatience for justice, which grows stronger each year among Aboriginal Australia. He says it is the 'torment of powerlessness of the downtrodden' that drives the current process of constitutional reform. Pearson observes that unlike comparable countries, such as New Zealand, Canada and the United States, Indigenous Australia has waited 228 years for the kinds of reforms we see routinely rolled out to our common law cousins and where the right to self-determination underpins the relationships between first nations and the state. With the election in Canada of Justin Trudeau, who put commitment to reconciliation at the front and centre of his campaign,

Australia continues to move, says Pearson, at a horse-and-buggy pace, in circles with no destination. He alludes to the 'tread softly' approach of the school of gradualism, as identified by other authors, that 'something better' can be achieved later.

Pearson eloquently refers to the plague of national 'nobodyness' experienced by our people, the 'airtight cage of poverty' in an affluent society and the depressing clouds of inferiority that engulf our people. On the 'symbolism is better than nothing' position, Pearson alludes to same sex marriage—civil union is a halfway house and there can be no partial recognition of gay marriage. Nor can there be merely symbolic recognition, a 'mediocre, tokenistic result' because of some overcooked and 'fanciful' claims that substantive recognition awaits 'down the track'.

Pearson's chapter sets out to re-imagine settlement and what might Indigenous peoples have negotiated for had they been at the constitutional convention table. He says our leaders would have spoken of power and control, a 'King-like exercise, negotiating power and freedom from a position of powerlessness'. It would not, Pearson exhorts, have been wasted on facile discussion of a minimalist preamble. Our proud tribal elders would have spoken of legal and political rights and the conditions for our inclusion in the union. Pearson argues that the Constitution is fundamentally about power and freedom and power is the correct test for recognition. He powerfully contends that our ancestors would not have negotiated themselves three lines of decorative effect in a document that is about distribution of power and freedom.

In the final section of the essay Pearson goes on to set down the technical aspects of reform he frames around the themes of rights, representation and agreements. In particular he explains the proposal, crafted in response to conservative objections to rights, to establish an Indigenous advisory body that enables greater Indigenous participation in the parliament through a dialogue model. This, he argues, would lead to a paradigm shift in the relationship between Indigenous peoples and the state. Here, Pearson mounts a persuasive argument for a declaration of recognition outside of the Constitution—a statute of reconciliation—that sets down the high principles that should govern the relationship between the state and Indigenous peoples. This would be symbolic given it includes the entire federation in a defining moment when the states, territories and the Commonwealth all commit to a new way forward, and because it is in statute it avoids the problems of symbolism in the Constitution including but not limited to interpretive consequences. Pearson concludes by viewing this process as marrying together the Indigenous, British and multicultural character of Australia. And a final opportunity to give voice to those routinely unheard and put into place measures that ensure the wrongs of the past do not happen again.

Marcia Langton's chapter begins with an historical overview of the exclusion of Aboriginal people from the Constitution. Then the story shifts from 1901 to 2007 and the meeting of minds between Galarrwuy Yunupingu, the elder of the Gumatj clan in north-east Arnhem Land, and Cape York leader Noel Pearson. Langton goes on to explain why race should be removed from the Constitution and why 'our peoplehood', which has been undermined over the years, should be recognised. Langton argues for a broadening of the understanding of Aboriginal and Torres Strait Islander peoples as first peoples, as recognised in the *United Nations Declaration on the Rights of Indigenous Peoples.* The importance of recognition as polities is a common theme in the collection.

Langton recalls a time when Australians understood the rights of Aboriginal people. Langton argues this is not the case now. It is more difficult now because, as Langton identifies, Australians today are 'race-obsessed' and the political discourse is not sophisticated enough to accommodate notions of ethnicity or polity or culture and especially first peoples. This is because the *sameness* that lies at the heart of the national identity is more acute than it ever was. Langton then goes on to explain that one of the consequences of this Australian sameness is the tyranny of the ballot box—the problem of all indigenous populations in liberal democracies. As Langton points out, with 3 per cent of the population it is near impossible that there is any accountability of parliament's decision-making. Her conclusion is that we owe it to the earlier civil rights movement to work out a path forward through the complexities and setbacks of the past four years.

Megan Davis begins her chapter by identifying the 'tin ear' of the Australian polity when it comes to Aboriginal and Torres Strait Islander peoples' aspirations. Like Langton, Davis was a member of the Expert Panel and is now a member of the referendum council and, as a constitutional lawyer, has monitored the process closely. She expresses concern for the resistance movement to recognition. These are red flags for any referendum and the solution will be to re-engage communities and reassess. Being so close to the process Davis identifies two roadblocks: the privileging of campaign tactics and the referendum statistics in the debate, rather than the principle and model of reform; and the Pavlovian response to any reform as ambitious. Listing the multitudes of processes over the decades, Davis suggests that the state creates forums to listen to what people have to say but those forums do not hear. We know this because all efforts at structural reform have failed. It may be, as Stauffer suggests, that these unresolved grievances are 'haunting' the sites of reconciliation. Like Langton, Davis identifies the sameness that is at the core of the current national identity that militates against complex and rigorously reasoned proposals for reform by Aboriginal and Torres Strait Islander peoples. Davis is frustrated that the state continues to ignore these proposals even though they are likely to be what is missing from the closing the gap agenda.

Kirstie Parker's chapter was written in the final days of her term as co-chair of the National Congress of Australia's First Peoples. Parker was one of four Aboriginal leaders, including Dodson, Pearson and Davis, who lobbied hard in 2015 for Aboriginal conventions as a critical step towards a referendum. Parker's chapter pulls no punches; as she observes, Australians generally pride themselves on calling a spade a spade, and her chapter does just that. Parker begins with a quote from the late Dr Charles Perkins, who also called a spade a spade: '*We live off the crumbs of the white Australian table and are told to be grateful.* 'Parker's powerful essay questions whether the groundwork has been done for a successful referendum. Reflecting on the 1967 Referendum, held on 27 May that year, Parker asks us not to forget that the day before is now National Sorry Day. From this, we 'have scarcely begun to recover' and while in 'recovery mode' we are in the middle of what Parker argues is an 'ongoing assault on our existence, our connection to country and our cultures'. This ongoing assault, as identified by Langton, Pearson, Dodson, Scott, Casey, Gooda and many others, is catastrophic. For Aboriginal people to be routinely told that an 'unsuccessful' referendum would be catastrophic for the national psyche and for the ongoing process of reconciliation is not especially persuasive to an audience who experience catastrophe virtually every day. The incoherency of the narrative, as illustrated by Parker in a series of bullet points setting out the facts, invites the question: 'Is government even competent enough for us to engage with?'

Parker pinpoints the federal government's disrespect towards the National Congress of Australia's First Peoples as speaking volumes. The 'gravely insulting' lack of engagement with the National Congress is viewed not only as a slight on the age-old democratic entitlement—chosen by our people for our people—but is disrespectful to the 8500 Aboriginal and Torres Strait Islander individual members and 180 Aboriginal and Torres Strait Islander organisations (whose individual memberships alone cover most of the Indigenous population), yet they expect the congress membership to respond favourably to a recognition process? The continual spurning of the national body—designed and conceived by Aboriginal and Torres Strait Islander peoples themselves—by prime ministers Abbott and Turnbull calls into question the value they place in the organisation and its members. In spite of this dire policy background, and although she is no longer involved in the process and no longer co-chair of the National Congress, Parker reaffirms her on-the-record commitment to the Expert Panel recommendations, 'what remains the most exhaustive contemporary consultation' to date on constitutional reform. Still much time has passed since those consultations in 2011 and not all communities participated. She is now happy to take a back seat and to allow communities themselves to determine the reform, whether it be a non-discrimination clause or a constitutionally enshrined body (that has as much 'grunt' as possible to compel parliament to take notice) or other non-constitutional measures. Like Davis and Pearson and Langton and Bourne and most of the authors in the collection, Parker remains optimistic; she is determined that the efforts of her late grandfather and her late mum and the past generations who stood up for our current and future generations will not have been in vain.

This is an important coda from Parker; the red flags emerging in the current 'recognition' process arise from the artificial attempt of the campaign to replicate the 1967 Referendum and the grassroots support of that c ampaign. It is increasingly apparent that successive governments are engaging in a process of outsourcing difficult decisions to more and more processes to decide the referendum question rather than showing political leadership. This approach, or 'elite manipulation', is an important hallmark of Australia's numerous failed referendums. The primary focus has been on the requirement for bipartisanship based on a crude referendum-win calculus, to the exclusion of the evidence base that Australia favours elite-driven processes over deliberative constitutional processes and this primarily accounts for the failure rate.

Tony McAvoy is Australia's first Aboriginal senior counsel. His chapter is a clinical analysis of what the ultimate outcome is for the Aboriginal political domain in its ongoing advocacy for structural reform. McAvoy argues that constitutional reform is neither a step along the way nor the ultimate outcome. It is merely part of the package. This aligns with many essays in the collection. The outcome of the package is the relationship between the first peoples and the state. As so many essayists have noted, the country was not settled; it was invaded. McAvoy argues that the fact of settlement is deeply ingrained in the Australian psyche. This was perpetuated by the High Court in the *Mabo v Queensland (No 2)* case, which created a 'halfway house' that made *permissible,* despite convention, settlement over the lands occupied and governed by another. McAvoy calls this finding the 'immovable rock' to which Australians are consciously and unconsciously hitched. Like so many authors in this collection, McAvoy identifies the answer to this as political not legal. Given the Recognise campaign has animated so much resistance and an awakening of Aboriginal demands for a treaty that would unsettle settlement, McAvoy argues, like Davis, that a referendum may not the vehicle to force this discussion.

McAvoy sets down a framework in which a politically negotiated outcome could be achieved. First peoples should be a part of the economic dialogue taking place in relation to 'future proofing' Australia's economy.

And like Langton and other authors, McAvoy insists on the concept of 'first nations' because this is where the cultural authority to make decisions comes from. McAvoy adopts a United Nations structure called the Assembly of First Nations, the foundational declaration being the settlement with the state. McAvoy cautions against a superficial approach to this—that the issue is done and dusted and the relationship will be harmonious. He draws on his extensive experience as a barrister in Indigenous Land Use Agreements and native title determinations. The reality is these are legal texts and lawyers will need to be engaged constantly and diligently to oversee the performance of these agreements. This has been the case with Canada and with New Zealand. McAvoy says that a treaty may not give us the ability to stop unwanted decisions in respect of our lands, but it should provide us with greater levels of control.

Asmi Wood's analysis of the current process of recognition aligns with several other authors: that recognition is only a step in a continuous journey. Wood is a realist. He is the only author to suggest a minimalist amendment, but his conservativeness is deceiving. From the outset he identifies what other authors have, and this is the inclination of first peoples to disengage from the process. Wood argues that the difference between the Recognise campaign and 1967 is that the 1967 campaign had the support of the Indigenous community. This presents, as Wood suggests, a problem in gaining national consensus.

Wood argues that the threshold of Indigenous constitutional recognition is where first peoples feel their position and status has evolved or improved. Yet he observes there is no political appetite for evolving Indigenous peoples. The political will to move the position of Indigenous peoples beyond that of 1967 is absent.

While others in this collection argue that legal recognition comes after an agreed political negotiated settlement, Wood suggests recognition even in a non-legal form may be a pre-condition for long-term solutions. Still, he argues that recognition in the Constitution is primarily about making Anglo-Australian law consistent internally. While McAvoy SC pinpoints the myth of settlement as being the relevant starting point, Wood argues it is that which was promulgated at Federation or the *grundnorm* that denied the existence of Indigenous peoples. For this reason he focuses on the removal of the races power. Although inconsistent with the legal opinion of the Expert Panel and the parliamentary inquiry into recognition, Wood is confident the 'current law' can fill the gap left by the race power or amended power. Wood correctly identifies the wish of the vast majority of voters to end race-based discrimination, as the Expert Panel and the parliamentary inquiry found, and as polling has shown, with the insertion of a racial non-discrimination clause in the Constitution. The ultimate referendum question, in his view, is to ask Australians to commit to equality of all, going one step further forward than the Expert Panel and endorsing a broad-based equality commitment.

While Wood advocates minimalism based on political will and referendum statistics, **Eddie Cubillo**'s essay is a compelling argument for why structural reform is the only acceptable path. As a Larrakia, Wadjigan and Central Arrente man, and a former Race Discrimination Commissioner of the Northern Territory, he speaks of the direct impact of parliament's suspension of the *Racial Discrimination Act 1975* on his elders, his family—a people who experienced the intergenerational effects of forced removal. Cubillo views racist legislation as an attack on his people. Cubillo says that the political class do not want a non-discrimination clause and the Indigenous polity want one. Yet, as Cubillo observes, that sophisticated debate on recognition is not possible in the absence of detail about what it will be. He raises similar issues to Sean Gordon and Geoff Scott about how the current policy settings have been 'devastating' and that the relationship between first peoples and the government is strained. Cubillo asks, 'How can we trust a government who is saying one thing, when their actions are reinforcing something totally opposite?'

Cubillo says the current process requires meaningful consultation and engagement, which is yet to occur. Cubillo says the National Congress of Australia's First Peoples is the suitable vehicle to co-ordinate real discussion and information flow through the Aboriginal and Torres Strait Islander community. After all, with

8241 individual members and 181 member organisations across Australia, the congress is in touch with a significant proportion of the Aboriginal and Torres Strait Islander population. The fact that the government does not engage the congress exacerbates the disengagement. On the referendum campaign Cubillo identifies a culturally appropriate process that is sensitive to a wide range of issues that could hinder participation, such as language (dialect) and deafness, and numeracy and literacy. In his experience, Cubillo does not believe that a constructive communication mechan ism is available to help Indigenous Australia work through the types of issues that will be central to the referendum and to have their voices heard. Cubillo also raises the issue raised by most authors, like Langton and McAvoy, that we are many polities and we do not agree on all things. There is disagreement and that is normal.

Like Marcia Langton, Torres Strait Islander woman **Josephine Bourne** refers to the *United Nations Declaration on the Rights of Indigenous Peoples* as an important framework for the articulation of Indigenous rights. Bourne says she is buoyed by the potential of the recognition project but she also cautions that constitutional reform and recognition must be meaningful and this cannot just be what Australians are willing to vote 'Yes' to. Symbolism may create a fleeting feel-good moment but it will do little for the protection of Aboriginal and Torres Strait

Islander rights and it can also do damage—an important point ignored by many in the debate.

Bourne, who was a member of the Expert Panel, writes of her Torres Strait family heritage and her grandfather's life under the *Aboriginal Protection Act 1909.* Bourne recalls the activism of the Torres Strait Islander people in the maritime strike in 1936 and in the 1967 Referendum. Here Bourne is picking up on another theme shared across the collection, and that is the importance of activism and disruption in achieving Indigenous rights in Australia. Most advances have come through the sustained pressure of the first peoples rather than being initiated by the state. Bourne describes how the maritime strike led to more autonomy for the Torres Strait Islanders. It was an improvement on the oppressive protection regime. Bourne also traverses the activism of the 1967 Referendum. The contribution of Torres Strait Islanders to the campaign, in particular the Townsville mob, was central. This is an important message to Aboriginal and Torres Strait Islander communities leading into the next phase of the referendum process: *we know how to organise.*

Bourne raises the issue also raised by Davis of how post-1967 things did not fare well for the Federal Council for the Advancement of Aborigines and Torres Strait Islanders (FCAATSI), the organisation that led the referendum campaign. While Davis referred to the federal government's rejection of aspirations to be achieved under the newly amended race power, Bourne explains how FCAATSI struggled in the aftermath of the referendum. Bourne, who has previously served as a co-chair of the National Congress of Australia's First Peoples, notes that the challenges FCAATSI faced are the ones that continue to challenge us to this day. It is also a caution against the suggestion that symbolism or minimalism will automatically equate to change—1967 did not until after protest.

Bourne concludes that the Australian nation struggles to see the value of certain things to particular groups. This is because the nation's story is not inclusive. Bourne sees the recognition process as an opportunity for the nation to practise shared values; highlighting the 'fair go' as a good value, she says it must be applied to all. Bourne points out, like many authors, that in the absence of a package or formal agreements that set out an agreed working relationship, tension will continue to define the relationship between the state and the first peoples. Bourne uses the language of collaboration and transformation. Like Davis, Bourne stresses the importance of imagination—let's not be afraid to re-imagine and rethink the way we do business.

Dawn Casey highlights how the current constitutional recognition process comes amid deep concern about the Land Account and the weakened level of Indigenous representation on the Indigenous Land Corporation (ILC) board. The ILC board and the Land Account are indicative, to Casey, of much bigger problems. One is the insecurity of statute. Another is the lack of accountability of the parliament for its decisions on Aboriginal and Torres Strait Islander matters. For Casey, a policy technician, Indigenous policy must be an astute combination of central co-ordination mixed with decentralised buy-in and ownership to be effective. She argues it reflects poorly on Australia that no government in forty years has got it right. Similar to McAvoy, Casey singles out the Australian psyche, specifically the idea that first nations peoples 'should know their own place', as the most significant barrier to achieving meaningful constitutional recognition. In the end, Casey says recognition must be substantive in order to compel change. Casey singles out the Racial Discrimination Act as an example of statute that *changes behaviour.* Casey says there is no guarantee that minimalism or symbolism changes behaviour. Casey calls for a mechanism to guarantee Indigenous rights and for some Indigenous power within the nation emphasising the structural reform that each and every essayist has called for.

Nyunggai Warren Mundine says it is too often overlooked in constitutional recognition that the first peoples have already been recognised through the High Court's decision in Mabo. Mundine also notes the equally overlooked fact that Australians have already been asked once to recognise first peoples, among others, in the 1999 Referendum and the vote failed. Mundine echoes many critiques of the current process when he says we still do not know what we are talking about when we talk about recognition.

Wrestling with the realities of referendums in Australia, he pinpoints an argument prosecuted in these pages by Langton and Mansell and Wood and McAvoy that the first peoples don't think of themselves as a 'race': 'The only context in which the notion of "race" is front of mind for us is the context of racism.' Mundine says that despite the massacres and the compulsory racial segregation and the denial of fundamental freedoms, Aboriginal and Torres Strait Islander peoples did not forget or abandon our first nations. Mundine observes that one of the first questions Indigenous people ask each other when we meet for the first time is, 'Who's your mob?'

The primary focus of Mundine's essay is treaty. This, he argues, remains unfinished business. He recalls the reconciliation process that Prime Minister Bob Hawke enacted when he reneged on his promise of a treaty. Mundine argues that neither recognition nor reconciliation can conclude its objectives if Australia does not revisit the idea of a treaty. Mundine argues that a treaty marks the end of a conflict, 'draws a line in history and allows signatories to move on based on a clean slate'. And to have any meaning, a treaty has to be between Australia and each first nation of Australia, nation to nation. Mundine says that while many people may think it sounds radical, that is because they are not well informed about the Indigenous sector, in particular native title. Mundine raises some similar points to McAvoy about agreements not being radical in the Australian landscape, mentioning Indigenous Land Use Agreements, which are binding agreements with governments, organisations and/or others regarding their native title and other matters. Mundine says that recognition was an idea of the Australian Government, not a grassroots campaign originated by Indigenous Australians, and what first peoples want is our rights over our own countries to be recognised and respected.

Like Asmi Wood, **Michael Mansell** is a supreme pragmatist. Mansell's chapter scrutinises the current recognition project, questioning the focus on the Constitution to the exclusion of statute. Mansell notes, as others have done, that this is at odds with the agenda of other Aboriginal leaders. As many authors in this collection note, there has to be more than simply a constitutional amendment, whatever that is. Mansell says there has to be more than reassuring everyone that *something* comes next without securing an agreement beforehand about what that something is. Indeed, Mansell queries that if constitutional recognition is only symbolic recognition then why is state-based recognition not enough? It is minimalist, symbolic and the states belong to the federation.

Mansell adopts a very legalistic approach to the Constitution—it is of a functional character and, contrary to what Wood argues, inserting acknowledgement or 'weak' recognition *cannot* alter the arrangements whether it intends to or not. He suggests that it would be business as usual. Mansell asks, 'What is the goal of recognition?' He describes the work of legislative reform as the conventional method of changing rights and responsibilities. Constitutional amendment on the other hand, he says, is anti-sovereignty. Furthermore, it costs an enormous amount of money. Like so many other Indigenous lawyers, Mansell has developed detailed proposals for reform, which he describes in the chapter. Mansell hones in on the Racial Discrimination Act, which the parliament has suspended, as Cubillo identifies, as problematic. Like many Indigenous leaders, the High Court's decision in *Maloney v The Queen* (challenging Palm Island's liquor laws) has made him question whether it is worth enshrining in the Constitution a non-discrimination clause if it imports the type of analysis set down by the High Court in six separate judgements. There, but for Justice Gaegler, the judges reduced consultation to what the government deemed genuine or appropriate. Mansell queries the point at which who determines what is good or bad for a community. Mansell suggests maybe the Racial Discrimination Act is no longer worth pursuing as a remedial tool. When it comes down to it, as ideal as a constitutional ban on discrimination is, Mansell argues that it is parliament still deciding what is best for Aboriginal people. The bottom line is this for Mansell: legislation is more specific and can be worded to convey the intention behind it and can be changed later. A constitutional change, referendum difficulties aside, is fraught with legal difficulties. As he powerfully concludes, who would have guessed the 1967 Referendum amendment would be used against

Indigenous peoples as it was in the Hindmarsh (Island bridge) decision.

Harold Ludwick recalls that, when the constitutional conventions were being held in the late 1890s, his great-grandfather was lost to the colonisers, and when the Constitution was enacted, his great-grandmother was sexually abused. He recalls the massacres at the Canning Stock route and Mistake Creek and Bedford Downs. Ludwick connects the time of Federation to the killing times: the frontier wars. This, he says, is the environment into which the nation was born. Ludwick argues the system of government set up under the Constitution is the problem, and that measures need to be put in place to 'ensure that things are done in a better way'. Ludwick pinpoints legislation as a problem. It can be easily amended and suspended and it makes Aboriginal people vulnerable. Like so many authors Ludwick draws upon the *United Nations Declaration on the Rights of Indigenous Peoples* and the right to self-determination. Australian law does not allow for fundamental rights, such as being consulted on decision-making about your life and community. The Constitution should, according to Ludwick, guarantee a voice. For this reason he supports a parliamentary advisory body. Ludwick believes that, if the parliament was obliged to listen more effectively to Indigenous voices, this would significantly improve the Indigenous situation within the nation. It would improve Indigenous lives in a real and practical way. In a formidable call for structural reform, Ludwick pleas, 'Please, allow us the space in your national arrangements to show you what we can do.'

Sean Gordon's essay links grassroots community work with constitutional reform. Gordon's chapter outlines the approach of eight regions to address the poor policy settings in place in Indigenous affairs to deliver greater autonomy to communities. Gordon says this approach is based on the right to self-determination and the idea that Indigenous peoples should be making the decisions about the laws and policies and services designed to benefit them. Gordon challenges Australian governments, saying that if they are genuinely serious about closing the gap they have to wake up to the importance of Indigenous policy-making, law-making and service delivery. For this reason Gordon supports a parliamentary advisory body that can facilitate Aboriginal and Torres Strait Islander peoples' participation in the parliamentary process and provide a much needed voice of first peoples in the laws and policies that impact upon their lives.

Geoff Scott's essay laments the policy environment as being at the lowest point since the early 1970s, with the Indigenous voice snuffed out. His essay argues that constitutional recognition, five years on from the Expert Panel, faces an uphill battle. Scott raises an unnerving aspect of the recognition campaign: the focus on the word 'race' rather than on the consequences of the laws. As others, like

Wood, suggest, the detrimental impact of laws cannot be future-proofed from the exercise of discrimination. This is why it is incorrect to say that 'discrimination' can be removed from the Constitution. If the focus of the reform is on a four-letter word that is not worthy of a modern liberal democracy, and not the *consequences* of the law (something Frank Brennan has pointed out when challenging politicians to revisit racist decisions), Scott asks whether embarrassment is a good enough reason to amend a constitution. Scott argues that amid the policy chaos the recognition initiative is in a state of drift and creating rifts.

Scott says the substantive proposals developed for reform are not surprising because each addresses a real problem. He says not being acknowledged as the first peoples is the *least* of our problems. In his essay Scott delves deep into the policy environment and identifies parliamentary accountability, given how vulnerable Indigenous polities are, as the major issue. Scott suggests ways the government can get the constitutional recognition process back on track, including ensuring the recognition process is truly deliberative and inclusive of community views and not manipulated or engineered by elites such as the bureaucracy. Scott's essay is not easy reading. He raises the many challenges we face as a group of Indigenous polities working with each other and engaging respectfully. Scott argues that if this is not the right process and not the right time, we should withdraw, regroup, rebuild and engage when the time is right. Scott proposes, like so many others, a negotiated political agreement that does not need to be constitutional. It may be the answer is not in our rigid Constitution but a document of good faith between first peoples and the Commonwealth. Like many other authors within the book, Scott argues that if we cannot advance, evolve or improve our situation from the current process then we should wait for another time. His is a principled position. It reinforces the idea that 'something' is not better than 'do nothing': do no harm.

Teela Reid's chapter is an important contribution from an Aboriginal youth who is graduating from law. Reid is one of the future Aboriginal lawyers whose opinion matters in the process that lies ahead. It will be Reid's generation who inherits the complex public law issues that have eluded the Australia of old. Reid begins by identifying the dual nature of Indigenous discourse on recognition—there is support for substance but there is also a substantial resistance movement. Reid begins the essay by mapping out for the reader the issues of race relations that have plagued the path to a settlement. Reid carefully and concisely maps out the problem with the race power post-1967 Referendum and why a racial non-discrimination clause was posed. Next Reid explains that reform should not be limited to recognition, however, and that Australia should listen to the ideas Aboriginal Australia has about how to move forward. This echoes the notion of ethical loneliness and the important role that those who have been wronged play in explaining to the Australian state what a remedy might look like. Reid begins with a treaty—a conventional and unremarkable approach in most places of the world. Here Reid is particularly highlighting the importance of agreed principles of engagement and mutual respect. This is important because it has never been done before in Australia's history. Next Reid suggests a bill of rights and provides a persuasive account of why a bill of rights is needed. The third step Reid lays out is a republic. This is an interesting approach and one not really touched upon by other authors. Reid has a very specific vision for a republic referendum, which includes designated parliamentary seats for Aboriginal people as well as a treaty. Reid is doing what so many young lawyers should do, and that is exercise her imagination on a vision of what she thinks Australia should look like in the future. Reid has effectively done what Davis in her chapter has said so few do these days, and that is approach law reform unburdened by political pragmatism and cynical polling. Reid is the future of Aboriginal and Torres Strait Islander Australia and it is important that she sees her future and her children's future in an Australian republic as a unified nation.

Nolan Hunter argues that the right to self-determination is inextricably linked to freedom—the freedom to be the primary decision-makers in one's life. The current situation is one where communities have very little genuine input into policy-making. This is why Hunter argues for a 'seat at the table' in Australia's democracy. Hunter is well placed to talk about this in his role with the Kimberley Land Council. The policy to close remote communities was made without adequate consultation. Hunter argues that without any recourse to any institution in Australia they had to resort to rallies and to the United Nations. It is true both of these fit within Australia's democratic framework, protest and Australia's obligations under international law; however, Hunter argues there should be a space in Australia for measured and rational debate and for nuanced policy discussion.

Like so many authors Hunter refers to the ways other jurisdictions have accommodated Indigenous polities. He points to the Maori reserved seats and the Scandinavian parliaments. He asks why Indigenous Australia does not have similar arrangements so we can have a voice in our own affairs. Hunter supports the proposal of the Cape York Institute for an Indigenous advisory body. This would guarantee us a seat at the table. Hunter argues that the proposal for an advisory body would provide communities with some power to have a say in how the federal parliament uses the head of power to make laws for Aboriginal people. Hunter calls upon other Indigenous leaders to take the opportunity to fight for a right to a place at the table in Australian democracy and have a direct say in the laws that are made about us. He argues that if we do not fight for a voice then, even after the referendum happens, we will still be in a powerless position.

The collection is bookended by the grandfather of reconciliation, **Patrick Dodson.** As every author in this collection has done, Dodson frames this chapter with reference to the deep historical grievances that linger from the unjust manner of Australia's settlement. And while there have been attempts to address the disparity in terms of socio-economic status, very little has been done to address structural inequalities. Dodson sees a treaty or agreement-making as a way to address those structural inequalities, but provides a caveat that this process of recognition may not be the vehicle to achieve that. Rather, this process is an opportunity to consider other substantive reforms, such as a guarantee against racial non-discrimination or an Indigenous entity to advise parliament. Although a treaty is the preferred approach, Dodson explains that it is something that can be done by Aboriginal polities with the state now and in legislation. Dodson argues that it is political will that prevents a settlement process occurring and that the treaty movement cannot be impeded by recognition.

Dodson argues that we should take the opportunity of the recognition process and reiterates the work of the Expert Panel, in particular around the crafting of section 51A, a new head of power to make laws for Aboriginal and Torres Strait Islander peoples, and section 116A, a protection from racial discrimination by the federal parliament. Dodson explains why non-discrimination was recommended by the Expert Panel, including the overwhelming support from the public for some form of protection from racial discrimination by the state. The Joint Select Committee on Constitutional Recognition similarly found strong support from the public for such a clause. At the heart of the advocacy for section 116A is that Aboriginal people have little cause to trust governments and the democratic parliamentary process. Indeed, Dodson highlights the recent debacles in Indigenous affairs that have created a dissonance between the rhetoric of recognition and the 'disempowering effect of paternalistic, top-down policy'.

Like Pearson and Scott and Gordon and others in this collection, Dodson notes the policy climate: 'communities are threatened with closure, sacred sites legislation is watered down and vital community based and driven programs are being defunded.' Dodson laments that 'in the absence of a clear direction with respect to constitutional alteration' it is hard to explain what the recognition might mean in practice.

In concluding, he reiterates that strong support from Aboriginal communities is essential. If communities do not support the proposal then there is no incentive to continue. This is why the idea for Aboriginal conventions around Australia was advocated by Dodson, Pearson, Davis and Parker in 2015. The idea is to hold regional conventions, gauge the appetite for reform and work towards a consensus on proposals. Self-determination means that Aboriginal people themselves must have a say in how their future is shaped. This means consulting first nations in distinct regions across the continent and the Torres Strait to get a fine-grained, nuanced idea of what recognition might mean.

Finally, Dodson warns that constitutional recognition is not a foregone conclusion. There are many obstacles to navigate. Dodson says that, while there is a need to be pragmatic, it does not mean we need to settle for a minimalist or purely symbolic approach. Dodson is nonetheless hopeful that if there is strong political leadership and a commitment to meaningful change, then there may be a referendum in the future.

***

As editors of this book and Aboriginal women who have served as members of the Prime Minister's Expert Panel on the Recognition of Aboriginal and Torres Strait Islander Peoples in the Constitution (and Davis now on the Referendum Council), we are optimistic about the process that lies ahead. This collection of essays highlights some of the many views on constitutional recognition. It shows that the word recognition is complicated and means different things to different people. We know that Aboriginal and Torres Strait Islander peoples can come to a consensus position on the way forward. We also know that the political and legal system we live in is one that respects difference and can mediate disagreement in a way that can lead to negotiated outcomes. This is a once-in-a-lifetime opportunity for the Aboriginal and Torres Strait Islander peoples to engage in a deep conversation with Australians about our shared future.

As editors, we also want to note that we sought to publish a collection that contained equal numbers of male and female contributors. Over the course of the production of the book a number of women could not contribute for many reasons, including work and family. We believe it is important to ensure that Aboriginal and Torres Strait Islander women's voices are heard during the process ahead. Too often aspirations for self-determination are dominated by a political agenda that excludes women's issues and women's voices. We hope that this process, especially the Aboriginal conventions, secures the full participation of Aboriginal and Torres Strait Islander women.

In concluding we would like to draw upon the vision of one Torres Strait Islander woman, Josephine Bourne, who adopts the language of collaboration and transformation in her essay. This is what we hope the recognition process going forward will be about: collaboration and transformation. This means collaboration between the first peoples and the Australian people, to map out a vision of hope and aspiration leading to transformation of the nation. And, as Bourne urges us all, let's not be afraid to re-imagine and rethink the way we do business in this country.

1

FINDING A RESOLUTION TO CONSTITUTIONAL RECOGNITION OF INDIGENOUS AUSTRALIANS

Marcia Langton

The exclusion of aboriginal people from the nation's Constitution took place in the nineteenth century, and it began with a speech by Henry Parkes, the Premier of the Colony of New South Wales. In 1889 at Tenterfield, he called for the colonies to unite and create a great national government for all Australia. At that time, Australia was six colonies. Each colony reported directly back to the Home Office in London on matters of state and was, in most important ways, governed from the Home Office.

Parkes wrote to the other colonial premiers proposing a meeting to discuss a constitution for the new nation, at which he famously remarked, 'The crimson thread of kinship runs through us all.' By this he referred to common racial and British heritage of the colonists as the basis upon which the new nation might be founded.

Parkes initiated a decade of conventions and public debate that culminated in Australian Federation and the Constitution in 1901. The Constitution was drafted at two constitutional conventions. Most people interpreting the Constitution today read about those conventions and the debates to look for the spirit of what was meant in the actual drafting. The convention transcripts and speeches are quite powerful in their impact on Australian society today. The main issues were the financial and trade issues arising from Federation.

At that time there was no free trade across the colonial borders. Each colony operated independently as a financial unit, thus restricting economic investment. By example, what they were considering was how best to weigh the interests of the small states against those of the more populous states in the new federal parliament that they proposed—how would New South Wales and Victoria stand against the smaller states? Most of the white settlers were in New South Wales and Victoria and very small numbers were scattered elsewhere in the other colonies. A key concern was that those colonies that still had large Aboriginal populations, such as Queensland, South Australia and Western Australia, would disproportionately benefit from the distribution of taxation income collected by the proposed federal government, unless Aboriginal people were excluded from the citizenry.

Customs, duties, tariffs and the capacity of the upper house to veto money bills were of far greater concern to convention delegates than anything else. No Indigenous person attended any of the conventions, nor did any delegates seek to represent their interests. At one point, one of the delegates proposed that New Zealand be a part of Australia, which resulted in complaints about including the Maoris, and the possibility of including Aboriginal people in the recognised population. Hence, New Zealand, the Maoris and Aboriginal people were excluded, the Aboriginal people quite formally so.

There was a long interregnum but eventually they made a fresh start with the 1897–98 Convention, at which they revised the draft. It was endorsed by the 1891 Convention. It was amended again in 1899 at a conference attended by the premiers and it was put to the people of the colonies of New South Wales, South Australia, Tasmania, Victoria, Western Australia and Queensland in referenda held between June 1899 and July 1900. It was supported by the majority of voters in each colony, but large sections of the community were excluded from voting, including most women and many Aboriginal people. Women were able to vote for or against the draft constitution only in South Australia and Western Australia, while Aboriginal people were able to vote only in New South Wales, South Australia, Tasmania and Victoria. However, even where Aboriginal people had a legal entitlement to vote, there is no evidence that they did so.

Aboriginal people played no role in the creation of our Constitution.

In 1899 and 1900 a delegation of the Australian colonies went to London to have the draft constitution enacted by the British Parliament. It was introduced to the House of Commons, completed its passage through the Imperial Parliament on 5 July 1900, and was assented to by Queen Victoria on 9 July 1900. The *Commonwealth of Australia Constitution Act 1900* came into force on 1 January 1901. Section 9 of the Act reads: 'The Constitution of the Commonwealth shall be as follows', and thereafter the Act contains the entire text of our Constitution.

It was the great Arnhem Land leader, Galarrwuy Yunupingu, the elder of the Gumatj clan in north-east Arnhem Land, who raised with me in 2007 his desire to see Aboriginal people recognised in the Constitution. He was concerned to ensure that the Yolngu people have a rightful place in the nation.

That same day, lawyer, academic, land rights activist and founder of the Cape York Institute for Policy and Leadership Noel Pearson also visited Galarrwuy and together we talked about how constitutional recognition might be achieved. As far as I know, Noel had never met Galarrwuy face-to-face, but had followed his activities because for much of his adult life Galarrwuy had served as chairman of the Northern Land Council, which was in its day a very powerful organisation. Galarrwuy was the interpreter for Justice Woodward, the Land Rights Commissioner appointed by Prime Minister Gough Whitlam in 1973, and learned from a young age about clan matters, the cultural history, heritage and landscapes. Galarrwuy was trained by his father to be the leader of the clan; his father was Mungurrawuy. It was Mungurrawuy and others who took the first native title case in Australia, *Milirrpum v Nabalco.* This was the case that laid out the flawed legal fiction of *terra nullius.* Native title was later recognised in 1992 by the High Court in *Mabo v Queensland (No 2)* (1992) 175 CLR 1.

Noel is much younger than Galarrwuy and he believed, incorrectly, that Galarrwuy was on the left, where Noel is a man of the right. Neither is completely true, as both of them are problem solvers with little regard for shibboleths of the parties if they do not advance Aboriginal interests. They came to understand that about each other but it took some time.

Standing on the sacred land at Gulkula in Galarrwuy's estate, Noel picked up a very large branch and asked Galarrwuy to hold the other side of it and push it with him, and they pushed it backwards and forwards. Noel said, 'This is what we have to do; you have to push from the left and I have to push from the right, and then we'll arrive at a solution that combines our ideas.' This idea of the dialectical relationship and its effect in allowing creative synthesis of apparently conflicting ideas has long been a source of intellectual inspiration in Noel's work. Noel thus began his friendship with Galarrwuy.

Following this, Galarrwuy gave two lectures at the University of Melbourne on the topic of constitutional recognition of Indigenous Australians and how the future of Australia might accommodate us with honour. He envisaged an Australia in which our legal, constitutional, economic and cultural aspirations could survive and flourish. The fates favoured his ideas during the final months of the Howard Government in 2007. Galarrwuy's visit to our University House staff club coincided with Kevin Rudd's visit and a brief discussion in the entry hallway sparked some interest from Rudd in the challenge of accommodating Aboriginal concerns. Jenny Macklin, who later became the Minister for Indigenous Affairs under the Rudd and Gillard governments, attended one of his lectures and was very interested in what Galarrwuy had to say. Some years later, Prime Minister Gillard appointed an expert panel to investigate the recognition of Indigenous Australians in the Australian Constitution.

I have worked with both Galarrwuy and Noel to ensure that Aboriginal perspectives on constitutional recognition of our peoples are on the record. As Noel and Galarrwuy do, I have my own personal views on constitutional reform: I believe that any idea of race and the ability of the parliament to use race in its law making should be removed from our Constitution. Because of the way that the notion of 'race' has been historically applied to Indigenous peoples in Australia, our rights to peoplehood have been undermined. I believe that our peoplehood should be recognised.

I am arguing that defining Aboriginal people as a 'race', as the Constitution does, sets up the conditions for Indigenous people to be treated not just as different, but also exceptional and inherently incapable of joining the Australian polity and society. The history of legislation and policy applied to Indigenous peoples demonstrates this in a number of ways: not citizens until after the 1967 Referendum, the shameful effects of the nearly half-century-old Community Development Employment Program (a work-for-the-dole scheme), the NT Emergency Intervention—and this is only to name a few of the exceptional initiatives that have isolated the Aboriginal world from Australian economic and social life. In response, many Indigenous peoples have developed a sense of entitlement and adopted the mantle of the exceptional indigene, the subject of special treatment on the grounds of race. My experiences across Australia over the past fifty years have impressed upon me how this exceptional status, to which many Aboriginal people have ascribed unwittingly, involves a degree of self-loathing, dehumanisation, and complicity in racism. Further, while continuing to be regarded in this way, Indigenous people are not required to be 'normal', which includes doing things such as attending school regularly, or competing in a meritocracy (except in the AFL and NRL and some other sports codes).

In the slowly building campaign for constitutional recognition of Indigenous people, it is vital that we broaden the understanding that the constitutional tradition of treating Aborigines as a 'race' must be replaced with the idea of 'first peoples'. By this I mean simply what is proposed in the *United Nations Declaration on the Rights of Indigenous Peoples*—recognising that 'Indigenous peoples are equal to all other peoples, while recognizing the right of all peoples to be different, to consider themselves different, and to be respected as such'. The next part of the Declaration states:

> Affirming further that all doctrines, policies and practices based on or advocating superiority of peoples or individuals on the basis of national origin or racial, religious, ethnic or cultural differences are racist, scientifically false, legally invalid, morally condemnable and socially unjust.

The problem is not race, but racial discrimination. Indigenous peoples define themselves according to their lineages and cultures that tie them to places and ways of life that existed long before colonisation. If we accept these principles of defining the status of Australia's Indigenous peoples, then the power that nineteenth-century race theories have had on our society through our Constitution and scores of legislative Acts becomes null and void. Not immediately, of course, but over time. This would not be a simple task, I need to say.

After the recommendations of the Expert Panel on Constitutional Recognition of Aboriginal and Torres Strait Islander Peoples were presented to Prime Minister Gillard and published in 2012, Prime Minister Abbott then made an unequivocal commitment to supporting recognition of Indigenous Australians in the Constitution. Several arguments were mounted against the panel's recommendations, and a 'No' case was threatened. If a 'No' case is formalised and included in the question to be put to a referendum, constitutional recognition of Indigenous peoples will almost certainly fail. In the history of Australian referenda, most of the questions that have had a formal 'No' case have been voted against by the majority of Australians.

Ours is the most difficult Constitution in the world to change. Not only do a majority of voters have to vote positively for a question put in a referendum, each Australian state parliament must vote in the affirmative and in the majority for a constitutional change. There is no other constitution in the world that is so difficult to change as the Australian Constitution. And as a result only eight out of forty-four questions in Australia's history have succeeded.

Some of us who served on the Expert Panel are concerned to ensure that when the proposed referendum question is settled, we have a strategy to avoid failure at the vote. If this question fails at a referendum proposed to be held in 2017, it will not be supported by any government in the future. A negative vote would completely rule out any possibility of this being taken up again in our lifetimes. Those of us who have considered this matter would rather leave it to another generation than have a failure now.

Two constitutional experts, Megan Davis and George Williams of the University of New South Wales, have published a book, *Everything You Need to Know About the Referendum to Recognise Indigenous Australians.* [1] It includes summaries of 'The Case for Yes' and 'The Case for No'. For the 'Yes' case they write:

1 The Constitution was drafted to exclude Aboriginal and Torres Strait Islander peoples from the political settlement that brought about the Australian nation.

2 It is important that the Constitution, the founding document of the nation, recognises Australia's full history, not just the period from British settlement.

3 We need to remove discrimination from our Constitution; it should prevent rather than permit racial discrimination so that all Australians are treated equally.

4 Recognition in the Constitution would protect against the future loss of Australia's unique Indigenous cultures which are a vital part of our national identity. Recognition will help improve Indigenous health and wellbeing.

5 A successful referendum to recognise Aboriginal and Torres Strait Islander peoples in the

Constitution would be an uplifting achievement that unites Australians.

The 'No' case is set out thus:

1 There are more important issues to address. Rather than changing the Constitution, Australia's politicians should focus on ending Indigenous disadvantage by way of health and education reforms.

2 Changing the Constitution is expensive; there are better things to spend tens of millions of dollars on.

3 The Constitution has worked well enough for more than a century; it should not be changed or tinkered with unless there is a compelling reason. If it ain't broke, don't fix it.

4 The High Court would be left to make sense of what the changes mean, and judges could bring about unintended consequences.

5 There is no agreement about how the Constitution should be changed. Even Aboriginal and Torres Strait Islander peoples have different views. Until there is unanimity, no referendum should be held.

These are the broad grounds of the debate as it is being conducted today, but there are more details to understand. One of those other matters to understand about our Constitution is that, when it was drafted in the nineteenth century, it specifically excluded Aboriginal people on the grounds of race, and it is this exclusion that lies at the heart of the state-authorised discrimination that continues to this day. Moreover, the Constitution authorised racial discrimination. Ironically, as George Williams points out, 'the change actually laid the seeds for the Commonwealth to pass laws that impose a disadvantage on' Indigenous peoples. [2]

A further matter that is worth mentioning about our Constitution is that it sits in a glass cabinet in Westminster, because it was created by an Act of the British Parliament at Westminster in London. Its preamble is a nineteenth-century concoction of imperial forelock-tugging.

In a more innocent time, Australians understood the proposition about the rights of Aboriginal people, although perhaps in a less sophisticated way. Australians voted overwhelmingly in favour of removing discrimination against Aboriginal people in the referendum of 27 May 1967. They were clear in their intent of removing racial discrimination. That referendum comprised three questions, two of which concerned the specific references made to Aboriginal people in the Constitution.

The first question, referred to as the 'nexus question', was in relation to section 24 of the Constitution, which required that the number of members in the House of Representatives be as near as possible to twice the numbers of members in the Senate. This section has the purpose of preventing the Senate's power overwhelming the lower house in the case of a joint sitting following a double dissolution election. The question was:

> Do you approve the proposed law for the alteration of the Constitution entitled 'An Act to alter the Constitution so that the number of members of the House of Representatives may be increased without necessarily increasing the number of Senators'?

This question was rejected by the Australian voters and did not achieve a majority of states in favour.

The second question concerned two clauses, section 127 and section 51(xxvi), which were the only references to Aboriginal people in the Constitution. Section 51(xxvi), prior to the referendum, read:

> The Parliament shall, subject to this Constitution, have power to make laws for the peace, order and good government of the Commonwealth with respect to ... The people of any race *other than the Aboriginal people in any state* for whom it is necessary to make special laws. [Emphasis added.]

Until 1968, the parliament could not pass laws for Aborigines because of section 51(xxvi); it excluded any law-making power of the parliament in relation to Aboriginal people, which legally included Torres Strait Islanders, of course. The second reading speech for the Repeal Bill—Repeal of Section 127 reflects the strange views of the time:

> Some people wish—and indeed the wish has been made clear in a number of petitions presented to this House—to associate with the repeal of section 127 the removal of what has been called, curiously to my mind, the 'discriminatory provisions' of section 51(xxvi). They want ... to eliminate the words 'other than the Aboriginal race in any state', on the ground that these words amount to discrimination against Aborigines. The power granted is one which enables the Parliament to make special laws, that is, discriminatory laws in relation to other races—special laws that would relate to them and not to other people. The people of the Aboriginal race are specifically excluded from this power. There can be in relation to them no valid laws which would treat them as people outside the normal scope of the law, as people who do not enjoy benefits and sustain burdens in common with other citizens of Australia.
>
> What should be aimed at, in the view of the Government, is the integration of the Aboriginal in the general community, not a state of affairs in which he would be treated as being of a race apart. The mere use of the words 'Aboriginal race' is not discriminatory. On the contrary, the use of

> the words identifies the people protected from discrimination. [3]

The other clause that was removed was section 127:

> 127. In reckoning the numbers of people of the Commonwealth, or of a State or other part of the Commonwealth, aboriginal natives should not be counted.

The majority of Australians voted 'Yes', and this referendum had the highest ever 'Yes' vote recorded in a federal referendum with 90.77 per cent in favour of amendment. So section 127 was deleted from the Constitution and the words 'other than the Aboriginal people in any state' were removed from section 51(xxvi). But, strangely, section 25 was not removed. It remains in our Constitution. It reads:

Provision as to races disqualified from voting.

> For the purposes of the last section, if by the law of any State all persons of any race are disqualified from voting at elections for the more numerous House of the Parliament of the State, then, in reckoning the number of the people of the State or of the Commonwealth, persons of the race resident in that State shall not be counted.

The Expert Panel has made specific recommendations for the reform of section 25:

- remove Section 25—which says the states can ban people from voting based on their race;
- remove section 51(xxvi)—which can be used to pass laws that discriminate against people based on their race;
- insert a new section 51A—to recognise Aboriginal and Torres Strait Islander peoples and to preserve the Australian Government's ability to pass laws for the benefit of Aboriginal and Torres Strait Islander peoples;
- insert a new section 116A, banning racial discrimination by government; and
- insert a new section 127A, recognising Aboriginal and Torres Strait Islander languages were this country's first tongues, while confirming that English is Australia's national language.

Former Prime Minister Tony Abbott said he wanted to recognise Indigenous Australians but, like the constitutional conservatives, rejected proposed amendments to section 116A that he claimed would constitute what he calls a 'one clause bill of rights'. At the time of writing, the views of Prime Minister Malcolm Turnbull are not known.

Most sensible people agree that section 25 should be removed. I wrote in *Meanjin* a few years ago:

> Section 25, which was not the subject of the questions put in the '67 Referendum and which

> remains in the Constitution, is more difficult to comprehend. According to constitutional law scholar Brian Costar, this 'obscure, puzzling, contested but largely neglected Section 25 of the constitution ... mandates not who should have the vote but how many House Representatives' divisions each state shall be entitled.' Some constitutional lawyers assert that it is 'a mild deterrent to discrimination on racial grounds'. [4]

Why would you use a race power to manage the number of divisions in the House of Representatives for each state? This smacks of apartheid, the hallmark of the old South African Constitution. Costar's thinking on this clarifies the debate for me, at least. He writes:

> At first glance then s25 appears racialist but on second glance one cannot be so sure. The section certainly seems to permit the states to exclude potential voters on the grounds of race, but also to penalise states that do so by reducing the number of federal electorates to which they might otherwise be entitled. Under this contemporary reading of the section, the constitutional framers emerge as progressive inclusionists: an interpretation, however, which is not borne out by the historical record. [5]

Costar presents a number of warnings, and two are: 'To assume that the Section has been voided by the passage of legislation deeming discrimination on the grounds of race illegal', and 'Furthermore, the right to vote is not explicitly enshrined in the Constitution'.

We don't have a constitutional right to vote, it must be understood. Costar writes:

> We can only speculate as to whether any future legislation restricting the right to vote on grounds of race, gender, class, etc. would be held by the High Court to be in breach of the 'directly chosen by the people' words of Sections 7 and 24. Given that uncertainty, a case can be mounted that Section 25 should be retained until the right of citizens to vote is unambiguously guaranteed in the written constitution or firmly embedded by judicial review in the unwritten one. [6]

Most people agree section 25 should be removed from the Constitution, but how do we deal with the explicitly race-based clause that provides the parliament's law-making powers? If section 51(xxvi) is interpreted to allow discriminatory treatment, there is a dilemma. We must retain the law-making power so parliament can make laws for Aborigines and Torres Strait Islander peoples, but find a way to prevent racist discrimination by the parliament.

This is difficult because many Australians are race-obsessed, and their political discourse is not sophisticated enough to accommodate notions of ethnicity or polity or culture or first peoples. So we have this problem that, for the parliament to make laws for Aboriginal and Torres Strait Islander peoples, we have to write it in such a way that there is an explicit power to do so, but which doesn't empower the parliament to discriminate against us as it presently can.

Noel Pearson devised an idea to resolve this dilemma—a dilemma that may yet prove fatal to our aspirations for our rightful place in the nation. He proposes that there be a simple constitutional amendment to establish a body of Indigenous people empowered to review all legislation in parliament and to comment on the effects of legislation on Indigenous people. This would, he believes, provide a hook for something more substantial outside of the Constitution, including a declaration of recognition that could then be legislated in the parliament, or could be a freestanding document. He envisages a proposed declaration of recognition having the status of the Gettysburg Address or, in other words, a founding document or a post-founding document. This may be the best solution to preserve parliamentary sovereignty and to avoid justiciable clauses in the Constitution—the two issues that are the grounds for objection by constitutional conservatives to the Expert Panel recommendations.

Because Indigenous people constitute about 3 per cent of the population, it is merely good luck that any Aboriginal person gets elected to parliament. As it happens, there are a few: one, and one only, in the House of Representatives of Australia—and he's the first ever—Ken Wyatt from Western Australia. We've had three senators—one back in the seven ties, Senator Neville Bonner from Queensland; a second in the nineties, Aden Ridgeway from New South Wales; and then Nova Peris from the Northern Territory in 2013. They are the only four Indigenous people who have ever been elected to the federal parliament. The state parliaments have a few but, again, this all is very recent in Australian history, so there's one in New South Wales, Linda Burney for the Labor Party; one in Queensland at the moment, Billy Gordon from Cape York; five in the Northern Territory, where 26 per cent of the population are Aboriginal; one in Western Australia, Ben Wyatt, but there were two until Carol Martin stood down; none in South Australia; none in Tasmania; and none in Victoria. We don't have much of a say in the parliamentary life of Australia, and we have almost no say about legislation.

To have a permanent body commenting on legislation would be a solution to the problem of our status as an extreme minority and our desire for a rightful place in the nation. Imagine the prime minister supporting the government of Western Australia announcing the closure of 150 out of 500 Aboriginal communities over in that state. The body that Noel Pearson proposes would lodge a report with the parliament giving advice on that proposal as to its impact on Indigenous peoples and other matters, such as finances, good governance and human rights.

In summary, little attention was paid to the details of the question in relation to Aboriginal people put to Australians at the referendum in 1967. The civil rights movement at that time was successful in achieving a major step forward in removing from our Constitution words in two provisions that excluded Aboriginal people from two parliamentary powers that affected their citizenship. The question, however, failed to mention section 25, which was intended to limit the franchise of people of 'other races'. The present-day Recognise campaign is focused on constitutional recognition of Indigenous Australians, as well as removing section 25 and other racist provisions. Getting rid of section 25 is a universally uncontroversial proposal. It is important for the nation that the referendum question proposal for recognising Indigenous peoples in the Constitution asks Australians to delete it. However, it is only one part of more substantive and positive recognition proposals.

The Expert Panel's report received widespread support for its proposal to remove the provision that enables the Commonwealth to discriminate against people on the basis of race. The idea that people should not be discriminated against on the basis of race, although receiving overwhelming popular support, is not supported by conservative constitutional lawyers who maintain the principle of parliamentary sovereignty and oppose the inclusion of rights in our Constitution. Their views will receive the support of the present government and will be most influential in the drafting of the question to go to the Australian people should a referendum eventuate.

Another proposition has been made by Noel Pearson in a searing historical and philosophical essay published by Black Inc. as a *Quarterly Essay.* [7] His idea of 'completing the Commonwealth' by recognising the Indigenous peoples, the British heritage and our modern multicultural nature is a compelling one. His proposal for including an Indigenous consultative body in the parliament to review legislation is an elegant counter to the opposition to the entrenchment of rights. The Canadian Constitution includes a 'duty to consult' in relation to first nations. It has proved to be beneficial to the modern task of incorporating first nations into the modern polity. Professor Megan Davis and I have noted in a forthcoming publication that:

> To many Indigenous Australians, Canada is regarded as a model of best practice for Aboriginal rights among liberal democracies; a kind of constitutional 'utopia'. This is because of the existence of treaties, section 35 of the Canadian Constitution in addition to the Canadian Charter of Rights and Freedoms (see *Canadian Charter of Rights and Freedoms* in *Constitution Act 1982,* being Schedule B to the *Canada Act 1982* [UK] c 11, pt 1). Also, Canada has taken seriously the notion of reconciliation in a way that Australia has been unable to. [8]

Pearson's proposal resolves the dilemma of constitutional recognition and the racial discrimination that our Constitution allows.

The unfinished business of the constitutional problem I have discussed here is the legacy of more than a century of history, but it is a challenge I believe we are capable of resolving. We owe it to the people of that earlier civil rights movement that set us on this path.

I trust that we will find the right question and achieve success in this most important endeavour: obtaining the majority vote of Australians at a referendum on recognising us, and giving us a rightful place in the nation.

There remains a great deal of work to be done to make Pearson's proposal palatable. It appears to be complex but a more thorough explanation, including a draft constitutional amendment and draft legislation, detailing what is proposed and what is not involved constitutionally and in statute, would bring greater clarity.

2

THROUGH BLACK EYES

Harold Ludwick

As an aboriginal person, my perception that I was at the bottom was well founded while growing up in the early seventies, seeing how our Elders were treated, when it was all too common to be subjected to racist remarks. Being called, boong, coon or abo. This was the entrenched racism that kept the inter-generational white superiority, and black inferiority, dominant and strong.

As times changed, it became clear to me that there is actually no difference between the white man and the black man. We are all human beings. We do not need to be afraid of each other. Though we are different, there is also much that we share.

Wantharra. Yurra Ngay ngani yiniil manathi—you see, this is one of thousands of languages in Australia, this is a real Australian language, an original Australian language. I said, 'Hello. What are you all afraid of?' You won't turn black by uttering the word *wantharra,* as we didn't turn white by saying the Anglo-Saxon word hello! Imagine if all Australians could share in the rich Indigenous heritage of this land, if saying *wantharra* was as common as saying hello, an Australia in which the Aboriginal person is equal to the non-Aboriginal, and the Aboriginal heritage is as equally cherished and respected as the British heritage of the nation.

In the late 1890s, when a series of conventions on the drafting of a constitution was being held, my great-grandfather was lost to the battle against the colonisers. The pioneers took our land to mine and graze their cattle. In 1901, when the Constitution was enacted, my great-grandmother was sexually abused by the white settlers. In 1906, when my grandfather was born, massacres of Aboriginal people were still happening—the Canning Stock Route 1906 massacre, the Mistake Creek 1915 massacre, the Bedford Downs 1920 massacre...

This was the environment in which the Constitution came into force. This was the environment the Constitution reflected. We were a 'dying race'—or so the whitefellas hoped. The Constitution had provisions that excluded us from being counted as part of the nation. It mentioned us—but with discriminatory references, ensuring we were treated detrimentally and excluding us as non-citizens. The Constitution provided no recourse for us to argue for our rights. There was no protection of our interests. There was no recognition of our humanity or right to be heard and to participate. We had the opposite: the Constitution promoted discrimination against us.

We weren't counted as citizens of this land. Some of this was fixed in 1967 when particular references excluding us were removed from the Constitution. But essentially, we are as vulnerable today under the Constitution as we were in 1901. The Commonwealth still has the power to pass racially discriminatory laws, under the race power. And we live in a system in which we could still be banned from voting—section 25 talks about banning citizens from voting on the basis of race.

We are not recognised as first peoples in the Constitution. Instead it refers to us incidentally as a 'race': the colonial concept of race that is tied up with ideas of inferiority. We were one of the 'coloured and inferior peoples'; invisible to love, invisible to humane respect. The Constitution condemned us for being BLACK!

This has had real consequences for our people, both in past times with massacres and colonial violence, and also in recent times.

The Northern Territory Intervention could not be challenged, because the Constitution says that the Commonwealth is allowed to racially discriminate! The closing of remote communities cannot be challenged, because the Constitution says that racial discrimination is allowed. The state law might be able to be challenged under the *Racial Discrimination Act 1975* (Cth), but what can we do when the money comes from the Commonwealth?

Those in power have the Constitution empowering them to enact tyranny against us: the most disadvantaged minority in Australia. No matter that we were taken to these remote places in chains. Taken there because whites did not want us in the towns. Our communities are so small, we do not get heard. We can be wiped out with the flick of a white bureaucrat's pen.

This is the problem with the system of government in Australia, set up under the Constitution. It does not give our people a say in our own lives. The majoritarian system of democracy has always failed to protect our people. We are only 3 per cent, and our voices aren't heard. Parliaments have never been good at listening to Indigenous peoples. This is why we are constantly trampled like our lives don't matter. Cape York people know well what this feels like.

In the 1970s, Queensland Premier Joh Bjelke-Petersen tried to legislate away Wik land rights through a policy to prevent Indigenous people from purchasing large tracts of land. The Wik people of Cape York had obtained funds to purchase the Archer River cattle station, part of their traditional lands. After years of court battles, the court eventually held in favour of Indigenous leader John Koowarta. They found that the Bjelke-Petersen Government's policy was in breach of the Racial Discrimination Act. It was a great legal and moral victory for Cape York Indigenous people. But the Queensland Parliament acted quickly to get around the court's decision. It declared the Archer River station a national park, which meant it could not be purchased. Years of legal battling proved ultimately ineffective in preventing discrimination against us. Parliament found another way to strip us of our rights.

Today, little has changed. Cape York people recently spent five years fighting the Queensland Government's Wild Rivers environmental legislation, which prevented economic development of Indigenous land. This fight was again led by the Koowartas, the plaintiff being Martha Koowarta, widow of the late John Koowarta. Last year, Martha was finally victorious in the courts. The court held that the Queensland Government's decision to impose strict development prohibitions on Indigenous land was made *without the proper consultation of the Indigenous traditional owners.* It was a great moral and legal victory.

But, yet again, the Queensland Government legislated around the court's legal finding. The government re-enacted the Wild Rivers prohibitions under legislation of a different name.

Cape York people have land rights, but through discrimination we are prevented from exercising our property rights the way other Australians do. We are prevented from using our land as an asset to participate in the economy. We are prevented from exercising free choice as how best to manage our natural assets. And so we are kept in poverty. Our people continue to spend decades tied up in expensive court battles, fighting discriminatory legislation. Yet even when we win those court battles, we cannot win the war. We are ultimately powerless before the majority might of parliament.

Parliament does not listen to our own solutions to our poverty crisis. It's our land, but we have no say in what goes on. *We have no say in the future of our people on our land.*

Little has changed in this regard since the 1970s. While the Racial Discrimination Act can be useful when a state government passes a blatantly discriminatory law, we have seen that governments can just as easily legislate around court decisions. The Racial Discrimination Act, too, is just ordinary legislation and can be altered at any time. It can be suspended, as happened initially with the Northern Territory Intervention. We are vulnerable because the Constitution provides no protection for our rights and interests.

Governments are not ever compelled to listen to Indigenous peoples before passing laws that affect us.

We argue for constitutional reform to address this.

Indigenous peoples should be guaranteed a say in parliament's laws and policies that affect us. We should be guaranteed a fair say in the democratic procedures, the outcomes of which affect our lives. The *United Nations Declaration on the Rights of Indigenous Peoples* enshrines our right to self-determination as peoples: our right to freely pursue social, economic and cultural development. Part of the right to self-determination is the right of Indigenous peoples to participate and be properly consulted in the government decisions that affect our rights and interests. Australian law does not allow for this. There are no systems in place for it to happen in a fair way. There should be an Indigenous body in the Constitution to consult with and advise parliament on laws and policies that affect Indigenous rights and interests.

The founding fathers of the Constitution guaranteed that the minority states should be recognised, given a say and protected from the tyranny of the majority, despite variations in their population numbers. Even the smallest colonies were recognised and given a voice in the system. But, because of the discrimination of the time, we were excluded. This must change. We too should be recognised.

The Constitution should guarantee Indigenous peoples a say in parliament's decisions that affect us. This kind of constitutional body is necessary to help ensure that, as Noel Pearson says, the discrimination of the past is not repeated, and that measures are put in place to *ensure that things are done in a better way.*

Our people occupy a unique place within the Commonwealth that is legally, politically and historically different to other citizens. We are the only group that was dispossessed and displaced by British settlement. We were uniquely discriminated against by the constitutional arrangements of 1901. We are the only group requiring legislative responses and solutions to this unique history (native title, Indigenous heritage protection laws, etc.). It is absolutely sensible and just that we are guaranteed a say in these legislative responses.

If the Constitution ensured that parliament listened more effectively to Indigenous voices, this would significantly improve the Indigenous situation within the nation. It would improve Indigenous lives in a real and practical way.

I leave you with a quote from Albert Einstein:

We can't solve problems by using the same kind of thinking we used when we created them.

The nation needs to change its thinking about Indigenous peoples.

We are not invisible. We are not inferior. We are equal citizens. We are distinct peoples.

We are capable of making free choices and informed decisions.

We are capable of having opinions about our lives and futures, and about the laws and policies that affect our futures.

We are capable of participating in Australia's democracy as equal partners with government.

We are capable of taking responsibility and leadership in our affairs. Please, allow us the space in your national arrangements to show you what we can do.

3

BUILDING OUR HOUSE

Tony McAvoy

One of the useful traits one develops from years spent litigating is the need to be clinical and objective about the facts, especially when they touch on matters charged with emotion.

Another benefit of being on the frontline of legal conflict is an understanding that one must be able to articulate with some precision the ultimate outcome sought to be achieved, and each step that is necessary to get there.

From my perspective, constitutional reform to provide for recognition of Aboriginal and Torres Strait Islander peoples is neither a step along the way, nor the ultimate outcome—if anything, it is merely part of the package that follows from the successful outcome. Nor does it create the space or set the scene.

THE ULTIMATE OUTCOME

In my view, the ultimate outcome is a relationship with Federation and the colonies premised upon the following facts:

1 At the dates of the assertion of sovereignty, there existed territories that were possessed and governed by our ancestors.

2 The territories of our ancestors were invaded.

3 The territories of our ancestors were not settled.

4 The territories of our ancestors are our territories.

Facts 1 and 2 are readily recognised in native title matters. Fact 4 is recognised in part. However, the opposition to fact 3 remains embedded in the national psyche. This much is reflected in, and perpetuated by, the High Court of Australia judgement in *Mabo v Queensland (No 2)* (1992) 175 CLR 1. In Mabo, the court disposed of the doctrine of *terra nullius.* But rather than concluding that we should be afforded the same recognition as the Bedouin of North Africa, the Cherokee of North America, or the recognition that the Western world extends to the West Papuans, the High Court created a halfway house that made permissible *settlement* over the lands occupied and governed by another.

The whole of the *Native Title Act 1993* (Cth) and the jurisprudence following Mabo is built upon the finding that Australia was legitimately 'settled'. That single pronouncement has proven to be the immovable rock to which the government, the populace and the Australian first nations have become consciously and unconsciously hitched. Further than that, too much time and too many resources have been invested in native title processes to now go back and make such a fundamental change.

Therefore, the answer must be political.

At present the national psyche is comfortable and happy with the notion that Australia was legitimately settled. There is no willingness to go back and examine this 'fact'. Mainstream comfort and Aboriginal discomfort with the largely inert proposal to insert words of recognition into the Constitution pivots around this rock. Mainstream Australia is not ready to agree to the objective truth. A national referendum to amend the Constitution is not the vehicle to force this discussion. The issue needs to be reframed.

While there are many paths that at first glance appear attractive as the shortest or surest means to a rectification of the record and building of a new relationship, I have narrowed it down to the two most probable, in my view. There is either:

1 a suitably enabled commission of inquiry tasked with the function of determining the:

   - precise nature of the asserted acquisition of sovereignty by the states

   - consequences of those findings, and

   - options to remedy any errors; or

2 a politically negotiated outcome that provides for final settlement or treaties according to a legislated framework.

Neither of the above options seems to be possible without strong and intellectually honest federal leadership and a desire on all sides to attempt to draw a line under the past injustices. Both options will need a mandated representative leadership from our side of the equation from which a willing government can draw confidence or by which an ambivalent or disinterested government can be shepherded.

It must also be appreciated that neither side will approach the options above without understanding the consequences. The consequences of recognising that Australia was not settled and that Aboriginal and Torres Strait Islanders have legitimate claims in an unresolved sovereignty dispute are likely to be land reform that provides for an ongoing process of return of traditional lands, compensation, equitable sharing of benefits, and appropriate levels of self-determination.

Ultimately, Aboriginal and Torres Strait Islander peoples ought to be able to choose to the highest achievable level of self-determination and progress to greater levels of autonomy as circumstances dictate. In the north of Australia, in those places where the majority of the population are first peoples, the natural consequence of dismantling the myth of settlement would be regional self-government. In the south, there will be gradations that may in large urban centres be limited to a recognised and effective role in government decision-making.

Obviously, the perfect time to hold such negotiations is during a period of economic buoyancy, rather than the present uncertainty associated with broad economic reform—maybe by the time we get to the pointy end of the negotiations the next boom will have arrived, maybe not.

Regardless of the economic conditions, a solid fiscal analysis will be necessary to fend off the inevitable claims that the country will not be able to afford final settlements. Indeed, we should be part of the economic dialogue taking place at this moment in relation to 'future proofing' Australia's economy. However, at present, no form of financial reckoning with Aboriginal and Torres Strait Islander peoples has surfaced as a contingent liability in any government budget paper or created a blip on the radar of the Productivity Commission.

Astute observers will have noticed that I introduced the concept of 'first nations' to the equation. I am absolutely convinced that the involvement of first nations is essential in both the process and the solution. This concept is not necessarily a perfect fit for each part of Australia, but it is intended as a moniker that can be applied to the essential landholding unit.

In the *Aboriginal Land Rights Act (NT) 1976* there is a reference to those who hold primary spiritual connection. In other parts of the country, a right to speak for country may be seen as synonymous with ownership. While the name is not important, the capacity to make decisions for and about country is the foundation upon which engagement with the government must be established. It is at this fundamental level that, as individual groups, we have what Mick Gooda, the Aboriginal and Torres Strait Islander Social Justice Commissioner, has referred to as 'cultural authority' to make decisions.

For the purposes of pursuing a national dialogue and a national approach we must come together as first nations with cultural authority. I have considered the various representative models that exist internationally and concluded that the model that best fits our circumstances in Australia is that of the United Nations. In general terms, the aspects of the United Nations that particularly suit the first nations of Australia are:

- the respect for the independence and sovereignty of each nation state;
- the adoption of declarations and conventions by a General Assembly; and
- a binding effect upon individual nations by domestic ratification.

For want of a more suitable name, the forum may be called the Assembly of First Nations (the Assembly).

The Assembly would necessarily have an executive council that would pursue the policies and declarations of the Assembly. I imagine that a foundational declaration of the Assembly would be that the settlement must be pursued between first nations and Australia's governments in a form that acknowledges and settles past grievances, makes provision for appropriate representation and engagement in the legislative and administrative decision-making processes, and provides for the implementation of appropriate levels of self-determination.

Without pre-empting the result of such negotiations, it is apparent that if we are to expect the states and the Commonwealth to acknowledge that our lands were not settled and their assertion of sovereignty is flawed, then we must also be prepared to concede that they have now achieved a practical sovereignty that is nevertheless affected by the circumstances under which it was acquired.

We and the governments could spend an extraordinary amount of time and resources attempting to determine the precise legal position that flows from an acknowledgement that the purported acquisition of sovereignty was flawed. I would rather spend the time and effort negotiating final agreements that make a place for us in modern-day Australia.

Aboriginal leader Nyunggai Warren Mundine has spoken of the need for treaties with individual first nations. I agree with his proposal in part. There should be treaties with individual first nations, but if there is to be any equity and fairness in the deals there must be a framework setting out the essentials for a fair negotiation process, and some minimum outcomes. The history of development on native title lands tells us that the outcomes to date have not been dictated by the value of anything other than the political bargaining power of the native title group at the time of the negotiation.

If, for example, the governments were to determine that they would negotiate with the native title prescribed bodies corporate (PBCs) as the representative of first nations' interests (a concept that is not without its difficulties), there are many who would simply be unable to cope. Even though the *Native Title Act 1993* requires native title to be either held or managed by a PBC, the funding of these artificial corporate constructs is so notoriously deficient that many, if not most, struggle to perform the basic regulatory functions foisted upon them under the Act.

It is in these two important roles that an Assembly of First Nations would have a significant and possibly irreplaceable role; that is, bringing the government to the negotiating table and making sure that the process under which individual nations negotiate is fair and equitable. There would be no obligation on any first nation to negotiate a final agreement with the government. Nor would there be any obligation to negotiate according to any framework agreement that could be signed on to.

FINAL AGREEMENTS

While the intermediate goal is to establish and enter into final agreements or treaties, it is appropriate to sound words of caution. Agreements with the government will not result in a harmonious relationship ever after. My experience with Indigenous Land Use Agreements (ILUAs) and native title determinations is that no matter whether the agreement is expressed as continuing indefinitely or the terms of the ILUA are set out in detail, the government will attempt to renegotiate, undermine or breach the agreement and engage in unethical practices such as nondisclosure of material facts, and disclosure of confidential material to third parties.

The reality is that wherever a native title group has a complex ILUA with the government, it will invariably need to have lawyers engaged to constantly and diligently oversee the performance of such agreements. I expect it will be no different for final agreements and treaties, perhaps even more so.

It is also clear that the aboriginal peoples of Canada have had to be vigilant in ensuring their government adheres to both the spirit and content of their final agreements. The Maori people will tell you that they must fight valiantly to protect their rights under the

Treaty of Waitangi. Irrespective of the fact that final agreements and treaties are never final, they are the tools by which we must re-frame our relationships with government.

This halfway world in which we presently exist is extremely damaging and unsustainable. It is far too easy for government, industry and interest groups to take small and sometimes large chunks out of land, culture and the right to exist in a state of independence. Take my people, for example. We were the subject of invasion, massacres, forced removal from our lands to Barambah (Cherbourg), Woorabinda and Palm Island. We had our language destroyed, and our ceremony outlawed, our children were removed, and we were forced to work for slave wages. Our lands were virtually given away to the occupying forces. We have now been told that of the meagre rights in the remnant pieces of land that the government will now recognise after 150 years of violent oppression, we must also step aside for mining and environmental outcomes. Every piece that is now taken out of us, and our lands, has a compound effect.

A treaty may not give us the ability to stop unwanted decisions in respect of our lands, but it should provide us with greater levels of control.

CONSTITUTIONAL REFORM

Once we have been able to push through the artificial ceiling created by the myth of settlement, constitutional reform will naturally follow to rectify the record. We will not need or want the platitudes that are currently being served by a nation that thinks recognition is some benevolent gift for which we should be grateful. Appropriate and necessary reform will follow. In my view it may be as simple as amending section 106 by adding text (in italics):

> The Constitution of each State of the Commonwealth shall, subject to this Constitution, continue as at the establishment of the Commonwealth, or as at the admission or establishment of the State, as the case may be, until altered in accordance with the Constitution of the State, *and for the purposes of their participation in the Commonwealth, the Constitution of each State shall be read as acknowledging that the sovereign status of the State is burdened by rights of ownership and dominion possessed by the Aboriginal and Torres Strait Islander Nations in existence at the date of establishment of the colonie* s.

I am not a constitutional lawyer and my suggestion is not a perfect solution, but no amendment ever is in this outdated Constitution.

4

TELLING OUR STORY, OWNING OUR STORY, MAKING OUR STORY

Josephine Bourne

When I think about the recognition of Aboriginal and Torres Strait Islander peoples in Australia's Constitution, three words come to mind: hope, capacity and potential. As an Indigenous Australian, I *hope* recognition in the nation's Constitution will add value and strength to the work that so many of us continue to be involved in today. The work I am referring to is the ongoing fight for the protection of our human rights and the recognition of the rights of first nations peoples as articulated in the *United Nations Declaration on the Rights of Indigenous Peoples.*

I hope that a critical mass and one day even a majority of all sections of Australian society are committed to building our *capacity* as individuals and institutions to uphold this work. I am inspired by the *potential* all Australians have to rebuild a nation that is far from the early days when our Constitution was written. A time when so many groups were not included in decision-making and leadership at the highest levels, a time when Indigenous Australians were considered as part of the nation's flora and fauna. Those days are behind us and that is where they need to stay.

Meaningful constitutional recognition and reform can only be achieved if all Australians understand the value of it. It cannot just be about what non-Indigenous Australians are willing to vote 'Yes' to. I fear that symbolic amendments could produce a feel-good moment for non-Indigenous Australians and do very little for the protection of Aboriginal and Torres Strait Islander peoples' rights. Similarly, meaningful constitutional recognition and reform cannot just be about Aboriginal and Torres Strait Islander peoples; it has to be something that other Australians can see and understand the value of.

There is an opportunity here to bring Australians together in a way that has not been seen since the 1967 Referendum, when 90 per cent of Australian voters voted 'Yes'. They voted 'Yes' to include Aboriginal and Torres Strait Islander peoples in the census and to allow the Commonwealth to make laws relating to Indigenous Australians. While we are working in different conditions with new technologies, social media, higher levels of education and numerous other social factors, this is an opportunity for us to figure out new ways to interact with the general public. Ways that allow them not only to be part of the education and awareness process, but also to support virtual or real space for critical dialogue. It's an opportunity to understand how leadership can bring people together and how people bring leadership together on matters that involve all Australians.

Recognition of Indigenous Australians in the Constitution is part of the long game in making Australia a great nation and it cannot afford to be dictated to by political cycles. We have to be willing to do the work, like the ten years of awareness building, education and collaboration that led to Australia's most successful referendum in 1967.

OUR INDIVIDUAL STORIES IN THE BROADER STORY

My grandparents moved from the Torres Strait region to the mainland of Australia in the early 1960s. They made the move some time after my grandfather received exemption from the *Aboriginal Protection Act 1909,* moving from St Paul Mission, Moa Island, to Thursday Island. After a number of years they moved to Townsville in north Queensland. My father's eldest sister told me that my grandparents moved to the mainland so that their children and grandchildren could have more opportunities for education and employment and to join my grandfather's eldest sister, who was already in Townsville. My grandmother's siblings and their children also moved to the mainland around the same time. Maintaining family and kinship connections is a cornerstone of Torres Strait Islander culture. In these connections are our knowledge practices and the important knowledge of how we look after others and ourselves.

As a child and young adult, I listened to stories told by my father and his sisters about their experiences of the move and maintaining our identity away from our homelands. I drew inspiration from their hard work, resilience through hardship and determination to continue to build on the work done by others before them—this will continue to be a source of inspiration for me. Similarly, I am committed to honouring their sacrifices by doing the best I can in my personal and professional endeavours while contributing to helping young Indigenous Australians achieve what they would like to achieve.

I am aware that so many Indigenous Australians are driven by similar experiences and no matter where we are from across this vast land there is a shared value of helping others who are fighting for the same thing. We are fighting to maintain who we are, our unique identities, our cultures, our languages and our connections to country in a constantly changing world. I also acknowledge that my own story and my family's stories are part of this bigger movement that so many of us have contributed to in so many ways.

Constitutional recognition is an opportunity to build a sense of pride and foster a commitment to telling the whole story of our past, transcending the will to avoid dealing with it, and recognising the obligation we all have to do things better—recognising the obligation to grow as a nation and being deliberate in our planning for the leadership and eldership that is required to make it happen. If we think about our own story or the stories of how our family or community contributed to building this nation, we will find survival as a driver, a commitment to growing individual and family capacity and the belief in the promise of our own potential, even if we only realise this in hindsight.

THE POWER OF ORGANISATION

As a mainland Torres Strait Islander I draw inspiration and guidance from significant political achievements in the Torres Strait region and on the mainland of Australia. Two significant moments are the maritime strike that occurred in the Torres Strait in 1936 and the 1967 Referendum. The maritime strike was the first time that Torres Strait Islanders came together in solidarity to fight for better working conditions and control over their boats. The strike lasted nine months and resulted in significant changes across the Torres Strait that gave people more autonomy. Despite continuing limitations it was still an improvement in relation to their control over their livelihoods and governance arrangements compared to the control government had over the region and its people under the *Aboriginal Protection Act.*

After the strike, the 1937 York Island Conference (also referred to as the Masig Conference) was a watershed moment for Torres Strait Islanders. It was attended by thirty-four locally elected councillors from fourteen islands and government representatives. It resulted in a number of resolutions concerning the improvement of living conditions of Islanders in the region. The resolutions related to more authority and power transferred from the local protector and government teachers to the locally elected councillors of each island. Other improvements included a commitment to building the capacity of the Indigenous workforce and a commitment to providing formal secondary education for the Torres Strait children in the region.

It was also necessary to reaffirm the maintenance of a continued commitment to traditional land rights handed down through ancestry, as discussed in Nonie Sharp's book, *Stars of Tagai: The Torres Strait Islanders.* [1] In more recent times, on 7 August 2013, the Torres Strait Sea Claim was successful, the biggest sea claim in Australia's history. Torres Strait Islander leadership is committed to conceptualising the management and economic development of the claim and continues to fight for greater autonomy in the region.

A watershed moment for all Australians was the 1967 Referendum. Over a period of ten years, a groundswell of activity and organisation culminated in the successful vote. In particular, there was an unprecedented level of organisation across Australia among Indigenous Australians. The Federal Council for the Advancement of Aborigines and Torres Strait Islanders (FCAATSI) in the late 1950s brought together a range of Indigenous and non-Indigenous organisations to collaborate on leading the campaign for constitutional reform. [2] And after the 1967 Referendum, financial resources were allocated to Aboriginal and Torres Strait Islander affairs. Local and regional organisations emerged to deliver services and advocate for the needs of Aboriginal and Torres Strait Islander peoples across the country. While the local and regional organisational activity continued to grow, organisation at the national level was being worked on as well.

FCAATSI strived to become an Indigenous-controlled organisation and they achieved this in 1973. However, with the emergence of other structural mechanisms at local and national levels, FCAATSI struggled to survive. In 1978, government funding cuts put more strain on the organisation, forcing it to cease its operations.

Despite the success of the referendum, since FCAATSI's conclusion, national Indigenous organisations and state-controlled national representative mechanisms have continued to face similar challenges. These common challenges include financial sustainability, lack of financial control, challenges in maintaining political relevance to a culturally, socially and geographically diverse Indigenous population, and issues of Indigenous ownership, control authority and power to govern the organisation independently. The issue of how Aboriginal and Torres Strait Islander peoples can create sustainable national Indigenous organisations to represent our interests and aspirations continues to be a challenge for us. Indigenous governance and organisational development is central to realising our own solutions for a range of social, political and cultural issues that impact on the quality of Aboriginal and Torres Strait Islander peoples' lives.

MOVING FORWARD

There is probably a whole range of challenges ahead in terms of process; I would like to highlight two.

The first is the need for multiple co-ordinating mechanisms that can engage with particular sections of Australian society. An example is the need for Aboriginal and Torres Strait Islander organisations to work with their constituents to raise awareness. Similarly, this kind of approach would be required for other groups. This work will need to be done in addition to promotion through popular media. Additionally, a set of practices will need to be developed for this kind of mechanism to effectively harness the existing intellectual capital on the subject matter.

The second challenge is providing people with the opportunity to embrace, own and contribute to the driving of the campaign once a model is developed. A key feature of the successful 1967 Referendum came from it being driven by a people's movement. The process so far through the education campaign Recognise has been a top-down approach. I do not think these things are insurmountable; they just need to be well-thought through by a range of stakeholders who are considering factors from a range of vantage points.

These next steps are a real test for us in how we are going to work in a way that respects and trusts what people bring to the table as well as the roles that individuals and organisations have in achieving the best possible outcome. This trust and respect has to be present from the local level to national level, and it has to be earned. To have everyone's trust is impossible; to have absolute consensus on a model will be impossible as well. I think it will be about communicating as well as we can the reasons why the model is what it is at the end of the process.

I see Aboriginal and Torres Strait Islander peoples in a process of re-building and re-structuring, starting with families, our communities, our nations. This work is happening with and alongside the native title movement and through a continued commitment to relevant longstanding aspirations and the emergence of new understandings of how things could work. I want to acknowledge the work that our people are doing across the country in re-building and constantly maintaining governance systems that are based on our knowledges—based on our ways of being and doing. As we know, this work of re-building, re-structuring and maintaining who we are—whether it is in remote communities, regional communities or metropolitan centres—is constantly challenged by forces from the broader environment that we live in and often instigated by government policies developed without the involvement of our own people—without the involvement of the people that it is going to affect.

I think as a nation we struggle to see the value of certain things to particular groups because we fail to tell our nation's story in an inclusive way. You only have to turn on the television in Australia to see that many advertisements still only have white faces in them. While this might sound trivial to some people, these things matter. As a nation we have so much work ahead of us in relation to telling our own story and owning our own story—the good and the bad. I have always thought that the value of giving people a 'fair go' is a good value, but it needs to apply to all Australians. Meaningful constitutional recognition is an opportunity to make a new chapter of our story and articulate and practice shared values as Australians.

Tensions between the Australian Government and Aboriginal and Torres Strait Islander peoples continue to exist in the absence of formal agreements with first nations. Formal agreements would set out an agreed working relationship and mutually agreed understandings of the status of Indigenous Australians. These formal agreements can take so many forms;

maybe we are creating successful models in some parts of Australia right now. I hope that meaningful constitutional recognition supports the resolution of these fundamental tensions. Especially in relation to a more collaborative approach to public policy development to create policies that support Aboriginal and Torres Strait Islander peoples to have greater autonomy over the economic development of their land and seas. As well as policies that support Aboriginal and Torres Strait Islanders to continue to manage and maintain their social and cultural wellbeing and rebuild and revitalise where necessary. My hope is that whatever model we land on, it is capable of transforming Australia in a way that allows Aboriginal and Torres Strait Islanders to continue the work of maintaining, re-building and re-structuring in a way that enables us to protect our unique identities.

Let's not be afraid to re-imagine and rethink the current state of affairs. I imagine a future where Aboriginal and Torres Strait Islanders have well-organised and self-sustaining systems of governance from the local level to regional and national levels. Where we have a multitude of representative structures that actually represent the diversity in the Aboriginal and Torres Strait Islander population across Australia. A future where we are all working towards protecting the things we all fundamentally value, a future that supports our own processes and dialogue to determine among ourselves whether we are part of a problem or part of a solution. I hope constitutional recognition enables us to build this future.

Recognition is a vehicle driven by hope. It is a source of inspiration for us to imagine our potential. It needs to be the expression of a continued commitment to making things better and a force that will build our capacity as a nation.

5

THE OPPORTUNITY AND THE CHALLENGE OF CONSTITUTIONAL RECOGNITION

Eddie Cubillo

Let's start from the beginning. The central question is, does the Australian Constitution need reforming? In my opinion, it absolutely does.

Why? Put simply, it's *racist.*

How is it racist?

Well ... the Constitution was written in the late 1890s against a setting of racism that led to the White Australia policy and a range of other discriminatory laws and practices. In short, the period during which the constitutional foundations of this country were established was also a time in which Aboriginal and Torres Strait Islander peoples were being dispossessed from their lands and resources based on the myth of *terra nullius.* Through both extermination and assimilation, Aboriginal and Torres Strait Islander lives, livelihoods and cultures were destroyed.

Given that this is the backdrop against which Australia's 1901 Constitution was forged, it is unsurprising that we did not play a role in its formation and that Aboriginal and Torres Strait Islander peoples are only referred to in negative terms. Section 127 even made it unlawful to include 'Aboriginal natives' when counting the number of 'people' of the Commonwealth. While section 127 was removed by the 1967 Referendum, other problems were left untouched. For example, section 25, headed 'Provision as to races disqualified from voting', provides that, if a state disqualifies the people of a race from voting in its elections, the people of that race are not to be counted as part of the state's population in determining its level of representation in the federal parliament.

The most controversial—and in my opinion, malignant—part of the Constitution, though, is section 51(xxvi). This section provides governments with the power to make special laws for 'the people of any race, for whom it is deemed necessary'. In the 1967 Referendum, Australians chose to strike out the words 'other than the aboriginal race in any State' in section 51(xxvi). While the referendum meant Aboriginal peoples could be subject to laws made under the power, nothing within the Constitution requires that these laws had to be positive. In effect, the racially discriminatory underpinnings of the race power, which targeted Asians and other 'coloured persons', were extended to Aboriginal people without any indication that the power should only be used for their benefit.

This section gave governments the power to suspend the *Racial Discrimination Act 1975* (Cth) under section 51(xxvi)—hence, it is called 'the race power'. *Kartinyeri v Commonwealth* (1998) 195 CLR 337 decided that the Constitution authorises the Commonwealth to pass racially discriminatory legislation. Basically this means that governments can pass legislation to the *detriment* of Aboriginal and Torres Strait Islander peoples.

The *Racial Discrimination Act 1975* has been suspended on three occasions:

1 to amend the *Native Title Act 1993* (Cth)—which removed existing guarantees of rights to Indigenous people;

2 when enacting the *Hindmarsh Island Bridge Act 1997* (Cth); and

3 when enacting the Northern Territory National Emergency Response (also referred to as the Intervention).

Suspending the Racial Discrimination Act under section 51(xxvi) to allow the Intervention took the retrograde step of suspending essential anti-discrimination laws that legislate against discrimination towards people who are Aboriginal *because* they are Aboriginal. This legitimised the views of those who believe that it is okay to treat people differently because of their race.

Since the Northern Territory Intervention this has been felt in a number of ways, perhaps most starkly when Aboriginal people accessing basic services, such as shops or otherwise, are subject to measures that apply only to them and demonise them as alcoholics or paedophiles. It is easy to think that I am overstating the point, but consider the reality of soldiers coming into small communities under the guise of an emergency. This is what happened. Consider what our Elders would have thought when they saw the convoy of army vehicles rolling in. One comment I heard was, 'This isn't a country at war.'

Not surprisingly, people in remote locations did not understand why the military was in their communities. But would any white Australians have understood if this had happened in their communities?

After the army came in, humiliating signs were erected outside of communities and people became subject to the confusion of income management under the Basics Card, which in time they found required them to line up in a separate queue in supermarkets. This brought back old and painful memories of segregation for many people.

I explain all of this because this is why the issue of racism and discrimination is so important to Aboriginal and Torres Strait Islander peoples. History is littered with examples of dreadful and systematic racism experienced by us. It's still occurring today, and we want protection from it.

WHAT WOULD CONSTITUTIONAL RECOGNITION MEAN TO ME?

I am a proud Indigenous man, from the Larrakia, Wadjigan and Central Arrente peoples from the Northern Territory. My family has experienced the intergenerational effects of the policy of forced removal of children of mixed descent from their family and country; however, I am fortunate in some ways in that my family has had the opportunity to be connected to country, culture and language through the *Aboriginal Land Rights (Northern Territory) Act 1976.*

I view the suspension of the Racial Discrimination Act to allow the enactment of the Intervention, the amendment of the Native Title Act and the enactment of the Hindmarsh Bridge Act, though, as an attack and an impediment to us moving forward as a people.

Colonisation has torn us apart as nations, making many landless, destroying our languages and devastating our spiritualities and unique histories. I want to acknowledge our Elders' struggle, their vision in pursuing their legal recognition of our rights to culture, land and the other legal rights associated with that. It has taken a long time, and I want to remind you that the struggle and fight for our rights to be recognised as the first peoples of this land is far from over.

I see constitutional recognition as an important part of this continuing struggle; however, we must acknowledge that changing the Constitution won't be easy and the path forward is less than clear. While potential constitutional change is mooted, we should keep in mind that only eight of forty-four proposed constitutional amendments have ever been carried by referendum. One of these times was in 1967.

Overall, it appears the substantive political sticking point with the recommendation of the Expert Panel on Constitutional Recognition of Aboriginal and Torres Strait Islander Peoples is the inclusion of a non-discrimination clause. Unfortunately, not including such a clause is, for reasons outlined earlier, a major sticking point for Aboriginal and Torres Strait Islander peoples.

It has now been more than three years since the Expert Panel's report and momentum for change has stalled because no model has been put on the table by the parliament. Until it is clear what people will be voting for, it is hard to do more than to be generally in favour of the idea, or generally against it. Beyond broad statements, any sophisticated debate is impossible because the landscape is not clear and the details missing. We also need to recognise that any constructive constitutional changes will happen only if improved understanding is built within the broader public. The information needs to be concise and clear. So until we know where the proposal will sit—pure symbolism, or something more—it is hard to have a concrete debate.

Furthermore, it must be acknowledged that in the current climate, relationships between Aboriginal and Torres Strait Islander peoples and governments are strained. We need to do considerable work to rebuild trust. But it is hard to trust when we have recently suffered devastating upheavals in Indigenous affairs, ecompassing a $130 million cut from the Tackling Indigenous Smoking program, discontinuation of the National Partnership Agreement on Indigenous Early Childhood Development and rationalisation of programs through the Indigenous Advancement Strategy, including more than $500 million in funding cuts. At the same time, the latest Closing the Gap report shows poor progress on improving the situation of Indigenous Australians on many key indicators. Meanwhile, in the justice space, despite ever-increasing rates of incarceration, Aboriginal Legal Services remain grossly underfunded and the Productivity Commission's calls for an annual injection of $200 million into the legal assistance sector remain unanswered.

This is the reality of the context in which conversations and proposals for the Constitution are set. How can we trust any government that is saying one thing, when their actions are reinforcing something totally opposite?

There won't be a silver bullet that cures all areas of disadvantage faced by Aboriginal and Torres Strait

Islander peoples, but real constitutional reform would have important symbolic significance and would ensure that our foundational document removes some of the racist elements that still pervade the Constitution. In order for constitutional recognition to be achieved—and for it to mean anything—I believe we need to begin a process of meaningful consultation and engagement, which is yet to occur.

I do not see this as government's responsibility alone; there is an important role for community and organisations to play and we should individually take responsibility. The National Congress of Australia's First Peoples could be the vehicle to co-ordinate real discussion and information flow through community and peak organisations to help build understanding and frameworks to assist the process of developing proposals from Aboriginal and Torres Strait Islander peoples.

I want to see culturally appropriate engagement with communities. In this regard, the proposal for Indigenous community conferences on the subject is an important step in the right direction. It will take considerable work, however, to ensure that real engagement and commitment occurs through that process. The feedback from community consultations has advised that for wide participation, issues such as language (including dialect) and deafness, numeracy and literacy need to be addressed. It is important that all members of our communities who wish to be engaged can be. This should include those who are often missing in debates of significance: Aboriginal and Torres Strait Islander men, women and children who are currently imprisoned.

Aboriginal and Torres Strait Islander peoples are seldom consulted in a meaningful way at stages of drastic policy intrusion in their lives. It is clear from my visits throughout Australia that a constructive communication mechanism is not available to help Indigenous communities work through this type of issue and have their voices heard. Having such a process will help us to gauge what the important issues are to Aboriginal and Torres Strait Islander peoples and models and questions could be drafted appropriately. This type of interaction and debate would be a good precursor for bigger discussions that we still need to have, including those about sovereignty and a treaty.

A common belief is that if recognition is delayed by more than three years, it won't come back around again for decades. In part this view is based on former Prime Minister Bob Hawke's moves on a treaty in 1986–87 that, while not as progressed as this debate, died after 1988 when he missed the opportunity. The risk is real and I can see the point. But, ultimately, I think that if reform does go ahead, it needs to have widespread support. This should be a process through which we can educate the mainstream on issues of inequality and historical wrongs, and which may build better foundations of fairness and respect for Indigenous Australians to help us resolve other issues.

So...

Would it be better to have informed consultation rather than trying to stick with a timeframe that won't bridge the divide of understanding on the issues? Do we need to go slow to make sure that we get something that is solid and reflective of all Australians? Do we have to consider all topics (even the difficult ones such as treaty and sovereignty), or do we continue to scoot around these like cultural taboos? Is the populace ready, educated and mature enough to make changes to rectify wrongs of our past as a nation? In all of this, we must remember Indigenous peoples are not all one people but many nations within a nation, who don't all agree.

Furthermore, there are a number of immediate issues that urgently need addressing, and which are in many cases more impactful on the daily lives of Aboriginal and Torres Strait Islander peoples. Would the focus and efforts on constitutional reform be better directed at issues such as justice, domestic violence, health, child protection and so on? Or, rather, does having these debates help build a platform that would better enable communities to deal with these issues?

These are questions we must ask ourselves. This process will have implications for Aboriginal and Torres Strait Islander peoples whether we have changes or not.

While acknowledging the importance of constitutional recognition, particularly in regards to repealing the race power, I am not really sure the country is ready to go to a referendum debate on such an important subject. I know that I need to know more so that I can make an informed decision and I am sure many others feel the same. I am not confident of a positive outcome for us, with what I see happening with government and its strategic attacks on Aboriginal and Torres Strait Islander peoples and key service deliverers.

In short, the current political climate doesn't give the Aboriginal and Torres Strait Islander community much faith. If we look closer, both major political parties have contentious policies that question our equality in this country. The Intervention and the Stronger Futures policy are both affecting my family members living on country as we speak.

We have wasted a lot of time—it has been more than three years since the Expert Panel's final report in early 2012 and now it appears we are being pushed to get a referendum without any real inclusiveness of Aboriginal and Torres Strait Islander peoples. I support constitutional reform as well as treaty and sovereignty. But without a question, we don't know what we are discussing and I'm not sure that the overall populace is ready to make such a decision at this time.

Aboriginal and Torres Strait Islander peoples need to make sure that they are involved in any development of the question and that their voices and opinions are heard. Thus far, Aboriginal and Torres Strait Islanders' participation is minimal and our input is yet to be heard or taken into account. Yet, despite the obstacles, the current climate of distrust, and the lack of informed consultation on this pivotal issue, I am hopeful that in time constitutional recognition will occur with the full input of Aboriginal and Torres Strait Islander peoples. It may not occur within the initial timeframe that we would like, but I believe that we must come together to change a Constitution that not only does not represent Aboriginal and Torres Strait Islander peoples, but also fundamentally treats us as unequal.

6

MINDING EACH OTHER'S BUSINESS

Geoff Scott

The indigenous affairs environment is an inhospitable, hostile and unforgiving one. Indigenous involvement in policy-making and monitoring is now at its lowest point since the early seventies and the Indigenous voice has been all but snuffed out. We exist in an Indigenous policy environment that is problematic and confused. We need to withdraw from the field and review where we are going. Recognition is not about us; it has become about non-Indigenous Australia.

The catalysts for the current climate can be found in a number of areas, including the perceived lack of progress in advancing the lot of Indigenous Australians—given the amount of money and effort involved—and the ideological differences between the current (and recent past) politicians, community advocates and the Indigenous community. This approach has been successful in establishing and reinforcing the 'us and them', the rights agenda or 'practical reconciliation' agenda, and the support or otherwise for the 'new arrangements'. The debate about removing the race powers is essentially a debate by non-Indigenous Australia about how they see themselves and how others see them. The focus is on the four-letter word 'race' as opposed to the racist actions of the parliament.

The call for constitutional recognition is an example of an absolute disconnect of Australians from the Aboriginal and Torres Strait Islander polities. We need to look at the current state of the recognition process, the obstacles to 'recognition', including current policy, and suggest ideas for how Aboriginal and Torres Strait Islander peoples should regroup.

THE CURRENT STATE OF AFFAIRS

The recognition initiative is in a state of drift and creating rifts. The reports of the prime minister's Expert Panel on Constitutional Recognition of Aboriginal and Torres Strait Islander Peoples and the Joint Select Committee on Constitutional Recognition have not been given the courtesy of a response from any government. In that vacuum, other proposals have emerged, all having merit, but equally lacking a response. The field has now become bogged down. The push for constitutional recognition to date has been a sorry saga in belligerent and mean-spirited politics. A project that should have been a positive development has now become divisive and problematic, with little hope of resurrection. Leadership is required if it is to get back on track.

The proposals on the table are many. They are unsurprising proposals given Aboriginal Australia's history. The call for a parliamentary advisory body is an attempt to counter majoritarianism. The advisory body proposal should have been expected given the lack of engagement between the state and Indigenous polities and a virtually non-existent relationship. The advisory body was not unexpected given the reign of the majority to the detriment of the minority. The Expert Panel's proposal for a prohibition on racial discrimination is unsurprising, too. It is born of circumstance: Prime Minister John Howard's Northern Territory Intervention, Kartinyeri and the Wik 'bucketloads of extinguishment' legislation have all served to increase the levels of anxiety and worry about the propensity of the Australian parliament to discriminate against Aboriginal people *because they are Aboriginal.*

The proposal for an amendment to the race power in the Constitution, section 51(xxvi), has attracted a confused and misleading opposition about reform removing the word 'race' but inserting another clause about 'Indigenous peoples'. To focus on the idea that race is odious, yet omit the actual racist *consequences* of a provision, whether it is called race or culture, begs the question in respect to the recognition debate: is embarrassment a good enough reason to amend a constitution?

WHERE THE PROCESS HAS GONE OFF TRACK

I thought the recognition process was an opportunity to encourage a greater awareness and understanding of the Constitution, a process to increase the awareness of Australians about civics. Alas, this has not proven to be the case. Aboriginal and Torres Strait Islander peoples need Australians to understand the Constitution. There is more to the recognition story than simply race is a bad word and it must be deleted.

A document was created to facilitate the Commonwealth of Australia; that is, the coming together of a number of colonies under a new federal entity, the Commonwealth. The document was created to enable this to become a reality. This document, yes, the Constitution, defined how the federal system was to be structured, including the federal parliament, executive power, the judiciary and the states; how the federal parliament was to be elected; and how decisions were to be made, what powers this new body was to have and what residual powers went to the states. If Australians understand the notion of how power is distributed legally and politically and the meaning behind the structure of the Constitution, then the notion of structural reform or changing legal and political structures is not such a scary concept. It is easier then to explain to Australians why symbolism or minimalism or gradualism or conservatism is not going to equate to any improvement to the lot of Indigenous Australians.

Instead of spearheading a civics program or better knowledge of the Constitution, the Recognise movement has become problematic. A government brief to raise public awareness has now become a source of division and misinformation, promoted by simplistic slogans and mantras. Regular polls tell us that a majority of Australians are in favour of 'recognition' and, even more unbelievable for anyone who works in the sector or knows Aboriginal and Torres Strait Islander affairs, that a majority of Indigenous people are in favour. But we are never told what the question posed is. What are Australians supporting? Are they supporting the mere concept of recognising, which is far from what Aboriginal and Torres Strait Islander peoples will support? The campaign and the polls are an exercise in smoke and mirrors, funded from the Indigenous affairs allocations.

In addition to these matters, I have raised the view that the advent of social media has ensured that any change will be difficult. There has been no referendum with Facebook or Twitter or any other form of social media. It is now possible to mount a low-cost, or no-cost, 'No' campaign—which has already happened—before a question has even been determined. The 'No' campaigns do not need to be formally funded by the Commonwealth—they are alive and thriving, initially from the extremes of both sides, but now from the everyday person who is sick and bored of the debate and now does not want to know about it.

OBSTACLES TO A REFERENDUM ON RECOGNITION

Before I discuss a proposal for getting the process back on track, I need to explain some of the obstacles to a referendum process, including the current policy settings. For some this will be new information because, but for a few senior journalists, the media does such a poor job in reporting on Aboriginal and Torres Strait Islander issues.

There has been considerable concern, criticism and misunderstanding of the whole of the government effort in the Indigenous affairs portfolio. This includes the role and responsibilities of the specific Indigenous affairs agencies and the line agencies.

The recent experiment to silo Indigenous affairs in the Department of Prime Minister and Cabinet has not been a successful one. There is no logic to picking a number of programs and amalgamating them into the Indigenous Advancement Strategy band, pretending that this represents progress. As yet there exists very little in the way of evaluation of government effort. Public pronouncements are about activity, not outcomes.

The recent Productivity Commission reports stating that the federal government will not meet five of the six targets of closing the gap bear testimony to the fact that the circumstances of Aboriginal and Torres Strait Islander peoples are not getting better *despite considerable effort.* It is time to assess and rethink the strategy. If we put to one side the consistent yet always rejected message from Indigenous people themselves, that structural reform is the missing and untried other side to the disadvantage coin, one of the problems of closing the gap is policy.

The responsibility for delivery of effort is split between innumerable agencies and the three levels of government. No one has taken responsibility for oversight or co-ordination of that effort. The lack of effective co-ordination and demonstrable outcome is not defensible given the level of funding over a significant period. Without an effective and efficient process for identifying the outcomes and progress made, this situation shall continue to be intolerable. These circumstances have led to significant tensions between all levels of government, between government and the Indigenous affairs–specific agencies, and in the Indigenous and general community. The lack of clarity and responsibility has caused significant misunderstanding and misinformation among the public.

There is ongoing debate between governments and agencies on responsibility, and an ongoing debate on cost shifting, which has contributed to the ambiguity and lack of accountability—a position that must be corrected if progress is to be made. I would be surprised if the proponents of the successful 1967 Referendum would have envisaged such lack of clarity and vagaries of responsibility so prevalent in Indigenous affairs today.

Each level of government and, in most cases, each agency, has sought to develop its own policy advice mechanisms: a committee, an advisory group, a consultative forum or process. While this could be seen as positive in intent, in overall policy development and focus it has proven to be disastrous. The result has proven to be unco-ordinated and unstructured policy development and ad-hoc unstructured implementation without any clear objective. The impact on the Indigenous community and individuals has been devastating.

If we are not clear on where we are, and where we are heading, or what our target is, the result is chaos. Everybody is very busy and there is a lot of activity, which may be efficient, but is it effective? Are we heading in the right direction? These questions should be at the forefront of our minds.

The level of disadvantage and the appalling circumstances still being experienced by Indigenous people today, and the pace at which this is being addressed, are unacceptable. The ongoing level of funding being applied to Indigenous affairs without the demonstrated positive outcomes is unacceptable by any standard. The question then is *why?*

Why are we in this position?

Are our policy parameters and focus wrong?

Are our priorities wrong?

How do we ensure that progress is made, is sustainable and makes a difference, a positive difference, to the day-to-day lives of Indigenous people?

The idea that policy development and decisions are the result of a rational and open process of consultation, negotiation and trade-offs, that seek to find an optimum balance between contending perspectives and needs, is a myth. Policy-making is a jungle that is very difficult to negotiate, requiring detailed insights, networks and knowledge. Policy advocacy requires a good knowledge of the area.

Only when policy-makers and advocates are backed by sound analysis and have an ability to argue with technocrats and specialists who have their own interpretation of the area shall we be successful. Policy advocacy must also focus on influencing the general public as well as a smaller number of policy-making elite—governments of any persuasion will be reluctant to act against public opinion.

The area of public policy is probably the most vital for the marginalised and disadvantaged in our society, because public policies are the product of competing interests. The debate is usually framed as a win–lose, with the stronger usually being the winner. The playing field is not level. The current political and social environment in Australia would confirm that not all sectors of our society are interested in eradicating injustice and removing poverty.

It is a challenge to the existing power structures and the structure of society if it seeks to change the status quo. In the end, the bottom line of strengthening the poor and marginalised is clearly political. There is some potential for positives to arise out of the future arrangements and some lessons to be learnt. Advocating for the betterment of a minority group is fraught with danger. In doing so you challenge the establishment, you challenge the status quo, you have to upset the comfort zone in which the majority of Australians reside.

The political environment is one beset by contradiction and denial. The debates and positions taken by players in the Indigenous affairs arena are, I would suggest, characterised by lack of maturity, frustration, ignorance, lack of evidence, opposing ideologies and differing priorities. What has made this environment so toxic is the lack of trust, lack of respect, and just plain meanness. The media has not been a commentator or reporter and provider of some analysis; it has been a frontline advocate for the Commonwealth Government, in particular, and for those Indigenous advocates who share the government's ideology.

GETTING THE PROCESS BACK ON TRACK

What is required to get the process back on track is for the leader of the government to define the parameters of this process: what is on the table and what is not? This statement will allow the necessary leader ship to be injected into the debate. Then Indigenous leaders from the many Aboriginal and Torres Strait Islander polities can make a decision about whether to proceed at this point and what is needed to persuade the prime minister and Australians of their own vision of reform. If this cannot be accomplished, then we will continue an inane process of smoke and mirrors.

The statement presented by Aboriginal and Torres Strait Islander attendees at a meeting held on 6 July 2015 with then Prime Minister Tony Abbott and Opposition Leader Bill Shorten on constitutional recognition set out very clearly what the bottom line was for Indigenous communities. This is a consensus view despite the many commentators implying that Aboriginal and Torres Strait Islander peoples will not be able to agree on anything. The communique stated, 'any reform must involve substantive changes to the Australian Constitution. It must lay the foundation for the fair treatment of Aboriginal and Torres Strait

Islander peoples into the future.' It set down very clearly what Aboriginal and Torres Strait Islander peoples regard as the minimalist approach: preambular recognition, remove section 25, and moderate the races power (section 51[xxvi]). The consensus at this meeting was unambiguous: 'the minimalist approach does not go far enough and would not be acceptable to Aboriginal and Torres Strait Islander peoples'. This minimalist approach was sensibly set out in the Aboriginal and Torres Strait Islander Social Justice Commissioner's Social Justice and Native Title Report 2015. There is no excuse for any politician or media outlet to not know what the Indigenous consensus position on constitutional recognition is.

If it is true we are embarking on a taxpayer-funded deliberative process that is in fact not deliberative because the elites have decided that structural reform will not happen and the minimalist position—acknowledgement, amend or delete and replace section 51(xxvi) and delete section 25—is the *only* position, this must be made public immediately. It is undemocratic and disingenuous to conduct a deliberative process that is designed to minimise citizens' opportunities to suggest reforms and ignore citizens' proposals for reform. It is equally disingenuous to design a process to minimise exposure of the Indigenous viewpoint to the Australian people.

Prior to any consultations, the government must provide this guidance. The conservatives have articulated at every turn that they will not wear any 'rights' in the Constitution—a fact reiterated strongly at Australia's Universal Periodic Review process held on 9 November 2015 at the United Nations in Geneva. If this was expressed at the United Nations, then it must be expressed to the Australian people before the consultations. It is true that many people will walk away now if section 116A is taken off the table at the beginning of the process, but is it fair to continue down this path knowing this?

Likewise the government has indicated its resistance to the prospect of an Indigenous parliamentary body in the Constitution—if this is not the case, then the time to make this clear is now. In terms of having a real and honest debate, the referendum is not about convincing just the Australian people, it is about the following hurdles:

1 the prime minister;

2 the government party room;

3 the parliament; and

4 the people of Australia.

The referendum process is driven by the elite, not by the people. In the absence of civics knowledge and full disclosure of the political machinations underpinning the recognition process, Australians are none the wiser. In the same vein as the political strategy outlined above, the awareness campaign Recognise is not a people's movement. It is a taxpayer-funded organisation with paid employees. The 1967 campaigners were a movement. Leading up to 1967, Indigenous people were unified. They were not paid a wage and were fighting for something—fighting for the Commonwealth to have powers to make laws that would benefit and impact them. Today, the fight is *not* for non-Indigenous Australia to *recognise* us. It is, as I have outlined above, much more complex. Recognise, for many reasons out of their control, has been divisive, not unifying.

HOW TO RE-ENGAGE INDIGENOUS PEOPLES

For Indigenous people, we will include in the proposals at our convention debates the imperative to do no harm. This would mean *do nothing.* This is always received so alarmingly by non-Indigenous Australia, some of whom genuinely want to do something. It is not the case, as some exhort, that something is better than nothing. Pursuing symbolism because it is easier to achieve and because of an unfounded theory that it will magically advance our lot will have a negative effect on our people. We have a Constitution that is very clear in respect of Indigenous people, and if that position cannot be advanced or improved by this process then we should leave it alone and not waste time and resources and political capital. We should leave it for another day.

It is disingenuous to urge communities to accept symbolism or minimalism now on the basis of an ahistorical theory of gradualism in Australia. Given only eight out of forty-four referendums have succeeded, why are the purveyors of this position so confident that a treaty or substantive recognition would follow in twenty or fifty years? Events in 1967 did not trigger government action on Indigenous aspirations or the reconciliation process, nor did the 2008 National Apology to the Stolen Generations. There are many who advocate for a treaty to be agreed to prior to any recognition being considered. This point has merit given the current process has done little to define the relationship and give rise to a proper process of engagement. Given the toxicity of the current environment, the only way forward may be to withdraw, regroup and enter into a negotiated process to agree on the principles that should underpin a relationship, one based on respect, honesty and goodwill. This is the challenge in front of us all.

DISENGAGE, REGROUP AND REBUILD?

There will only be one go at getting this right. I would strongly suggest that the time now is not right and we should withdraw from the field and await a better time. The governments over the past two decades have not acted with goodwill nor good faith in respect of Indigenous Australia, and the environment is beset by duplicatory bureaucrats, and ministers whose only responses have been indolent and paternal and focused on a range of interventions, not development, which has been a palliative approach resulting in greater not less dependence and therefore never-ending.

We may have to wait for the dawn of a time when government moves from ideology and paternal approaches to a developmental approach that puts people at the centre of the engagement. The continued failure of governments to respond appropriately to the dire situation of Indigenous people and the failure to progress fuels the frustration and sense of urgency that is felt by many Indigenous people. These circumstances are exacerbated by the ongoing legislative and operational actions of government to impose continuing and increasing 'administrative, procedural costs' and 'strategies and initiatives' that are effectively undermining the capacity to deliver real and durable benefit to Indigenous people.

Indigenous people must unify in action to ensure that citizenship and inherent Indigenous rights are secured and delivered. We must ensure that these benefits are delivered in a sustainable manner to secure the essential conditions required for the health and wellbeing of Indigenous people. We must support our own political organisation and capacity and not be dependent on the benevolence of government. That has been our collective failure in the past.

One of the most disturbing developments of the past ten years—effectively the government ethos—is to reduce people to the status of beggars in their own land as a prerequisite for receiving assistance. This is not a development that any fair-minded person could support. The driver of these developments cannot be social commentators, but Indigenous people themselves.

Indigenous people must abandon the tall poppy syndrome and instead acknowledge and celebrate our intellectuals, our thinkers. They are the people who can take us forward. We must be able to be organised enough and brave enough to take on the government and others to advance the wellbeing, the future of Indigenous people. We must match their technocrats.

We must embark on the strategy to build the capacity of our own, identify, support and educate people from our own ranks to take the fight forward to advance the circumstances of our children. We cannot rely on public servants to be a brake on the excesses of the political masters of the day. Recent changes and the 'new' operational ethos of the public service have reduced it to a mere shadow of the former professional body it once was; it is now devoid of the capacity for open, fearless and frank advice; it now cannot be trusted.

At the same time, we must challenge the taboos, the conventions and the ongoing failures in our own communities. We must challenge the inappropriate behaviours and activities permeating many of our 'communities' and 'organisations'—these must be identified and dealt with firmly and decisively. If we do not do this, others will have to. If someone does not have the skills or abilities to carry out the duties and responsibilities entrusted to them, then we must act, whether that is to provide support and assistance or to replace them. We must not shirk that responsibility. At the same time, we must be cognisant of the way the sets of behaviours have developed, and why they have been allowed to persist. In saying this, we must not allow ourselves to sink to the active business of degrading and humiliating people in this process. Any process of change must be based on the ethics of not to humiliate, not to degrade, not to treat with disdain, and at the same time acknowledge the efforts of many over many years.

The environment in which we now exist is one that is permeated by meanness, misinformation and the destruction of structures and groups that have achieved much—perhaps not as much as we would all like, but this lack of progress is a burden we all share. Indigenous community and culture is not rocket science. It is about identity, it is about connection, it is about reciprocity, about respect, and most importantly it is about collective support and unity. It can only be sustained where we all *mind each other's business,* and to mind each other's business is the very antithesis of a working contemporary culture.

We must continue to focus on ensuring that there are appropriate checks and balances within our society. The law should provide such a foundation, but in recent decades this necessary component has fallen short of what we all should insist on. The persistent and systematic undermining of our justice system should send a chill up the spine of anyone who values a society that cares for its members.

The excesses of the political sector must be of concern. We need to ensure that the accountabilities and balances are introduced into our lives, the necessary advancement on our current civil society where the rights of the citizens are balanced with rights of the state. The only right of the state is to act in the best interests of all its citizens, not in the interest of some sectors to the detriment of others—a difficult and ongoing balancing act.

The issues and matters I have referred to are not exhaustive and therefore in no way complete, but an attempt to identify the strategic and sometimes difficult issues we all face. We must come together and identify the priority and a pathway forward. It is our responsibility and that is why we are in the positions we now hold—each of us has a role to play. We must view the glass as half full, not half empty. If we wish to engage in the debate, it is not good enough to only criticise, we must also offer solutions, our ideas—our responsibility is to contribute.

PUSHING DOWN OBSTACLES

Working and being involved in Indigenous affairs is thought by many to be an insurmountable task, frustrating and heart-wrenching, where the issues to be resolved and the obstacles to be overcome seem to multiply as we progress. The truth is there is still a long, long way to go, but we should stop at times and look behind, to see how far we have come, to take pride and take heart in the achievements to date. Everyone must do their bit—those who work in government and those who work in the community or society itself.

The tone and level of debate surrounding native title over the past two decades confirm that today we live in a society where positive acts of denial, of misinformation, of division and of disrespect are commonplace and in fact permeate the ethics of many of our 'leaders'. Only with considered and responsible debate without the scaremongering of the past can we move on.

Indigenous people aggrieved by the denial of rights will seek a remedy—to their situation, to their plight—from other sources. The action in the international arena, notably the United Nations, is just one that should have been expected in a democracy which so poorly accommodates its Indigenous populations. There are calls by a few, a hope by a few, for everyone to be treated equally. This call suggests either of two premises: that all people are equal, or that inequality is the objective. To treat unequal people equally is to institutionalise and entrench inequality and in turn to impose division and disunity. This goes to the heart of the debate concerning substantive and formal equality.

Substantive equality is not concerned with simply treating all people the same; rather, it is based on the understanding that all people are not the same and that these differences need to be appropriately acknowledged and responded to. Australians intuitively get that our appreciation of social services pre-dates the United Nations human rights framework. Today we still commit to the principles of universal healthcare and social housing and a welfare net, even as the political elites try to chip away at that.

There must be a change in our stance towards society's less fortunate, those not enjoying the benefits that this country has on offer, and importantly reduce the thresholds for inclusion of communities in the development of policy and taking seriously what they say, what they think, what they know and what they need and their capabilities. If we cannot make that change out of the current process, we should wait for a time when men and women of good faith and goodwill occupy the positions of influence and decision-making benches of parliament, as they did in the past and hopefully will again in the future.

7

SHIPS THAT PASS IN THE NIGHT

Megan Davis

Having been involved in constitutional legal scholarship for a decade, I have been astonished by the tin ear of the Australian polity when it comes to Aboriginal and Torres Strait Islander peoples' aspirations. From constitutional commissions to parliamentary inquiries to reconciliation councils to expert panels to referendum councils, not a decade goes by where Australia is not aware of the need to address the situation of the first peoples. Yet all efforts have failed.

Reform is routinely stifled, being accused of many things from radical, ambitious and overreaching to violating equality or violating the *sameness* that is at the core of the national identity. Ten years on from the abolition of the Aboriginal and Torres Strait Islander Commission (ATSIC), the community is subject to what academic Marcia Langton labels 'the most incompetent and damaging experiment in Indigenous affairs' and what Aboriginal and Torres Strait Islander Social Justice Commissioner Mick Gooda describes as 'one of the largest scale "upheavals" of Aboriginal and

Torres Strait Islander affairs', yet still structural reform is eschewed.

There is nothing special about the predictable and well-rehearsed roadblocks in this current, elongated period of constitutional reform; however, the visceral response of the to-be-recognised polity, ranging from resistance to ambivalence, does make this iteration somewhat unique. *Can you have 'recognition' if the purported subjects of recognition do not want it?* This question, like so many things in the current era of proposed constitutional reform, depends on whether the state *hears,* not just listens, to what it is that Aboriginal and Torres Strait Islander peoples are saying.

The Indigenous rights recognised in law today were hard fought and hard won over the decades through Indigenous activism or Indigenous litigation. In many of those situations the state was compelled to listen but did not hear, resulting in residual resentment, a not uncommon by-product of an asymmetric relationship. As a participant in and observer of the current recognition project, the process so far is best described as ships that pass in the night.

Why do Aboriginal and Torres Strait Islander peoples pursue structural reform despite the challenges of retro-fitting accommodation and recognition so far after colonisation? What are some of the red flags in the current process and what could be the framework for reform?

THE PERILS OF PATRONISING ABORIGINAL PEOPLE

There are two things you should never say to an Aboriginal person about constitutional recognition. One is to dismiss our aspirations as 'ambitious'. The second is to knowingly cite Australia's referendum statistics—only eight out of forty-four referenda have succeeded—and gaze piteously at the thought of such a Sisyphean task.

On the first point, *anything* is ambitious for the Australian polity given the current era of non-reform. It has been almost forty years since the last successful amendment and almost twenty years since the last attempt—and let's face it, of the eight successful referenda (1906, 1910, 1928, 1946, 1967 and 1977), three amendments (1977) were at the same ballot, making the record even more unattractive.

The Constitution is a rigid document. Not all constitutions are so rigid. It is rigid because it requires a majority of states and a national majority for an amendment to succeed. Other constitutions are more flexible; for example, requiring a majority of both houses of parliament. It so happens that we live on the continent that was colonised by a polity that both chose not to enter into a treaty *and* drafted the world's most difficult-to-change constitution. It is what it is. But ambitious is only an apt description if the

Constitution is regarded as the *only* way to address unfinished business. And it is not.

The second thing to avoid telling Aboriginal people is the statistics on unsuccessful referenda. You are probably the tenth person that week to do so. On this matter, I have noticed among even my own students this contagious cynicism about law and policy reform. The referendum record combined with the Australian era of multiple reform reviews but little actual reform has created a generation of young Australians, baby lawyers at least, who dare not dream. My doctoral supervisor, Professor Hilary Charlesworth, once told me that the most important thing we can do as legal scholars is to exercise our imagination, to imagine the world as a better place and to set about achieving that. The many Aboriginal polities of this country continue, against all odds, to exercise their imaginations and conceive of reform ideas, to imagine that Australia can be a better, more accommodating version of itself. We survived frontier wars, we survived compulsory racial segregation; a near-impossible-to-amend Constitution is hardly a deterrent.

Put simply, the challenge of structural reform is that it requires a redistribution of public power. It requires the state to make room for Aboriginal and Torres Strait Islander peoples. This is why the state so often eschews the structural in favour of the gestural. The apology is a good example of this. There is residual resentment in the community that the apology was not accompanied, as it should have been, by compensation. To cherry-pick international best practice on reparation for gross violations of human rights, rejecting compensation for the wrong is, for many, unforgivable. There is an inkling of this in the how-low-can-you-go vibe to recognition, where the goal is not to fix a problem, but how to game the system.

It was my experience as a member of the prime minister's Expert Panel on Constitutional Recognition of Aboriginal and Torres Strait Islander Peoples that Australians wanted something big to happen; not token and not symbolic. Their words, not mine. But representative democracies are funny things. The will of the people is filtered through individuals, privileged enough to be chosen by the people to represent them. And that population's views are then filtered through a political party and subject to party discipline. It means on occasions there is a fair chance of dissonance between the people and the parties. The Iraq War in 2003 is a good example of this, and the public response to the proposed amendment of section 18C of the *Racial Discrimination Act 1975* is another. It may be that, when the Expert Panel undertook their consultations in 2011, there was optimism; closing the gap was fresh in everyone's mind, as was the Apology to the Stolen Generations, and we were in the midst of a mining boom. Today, we are post–global financial crisis and post–Paris, Beirut,

Indonesia and Burkina Faso terrorist attacks. Perhaps the mood of the nation is not so buoyant.

There are two issues that need to be raised before positing a framework. One is the assertion that a minimalist or even symbolic amendment can be leveraged for more reform. The second issue is the risk of reinventing the wheel. I will take each in turn.

One of the nascent arguments to counteract the Indigenous advocacy for substantive reform is that 1967 was only minor, minimalist reform, and because so much was achieved as a consequence of the amended race power then this can and should be replicated in this reform process. The 1967 Referendum provided the Commonwealth with the power to make laws for Aboriginal and Torres Strait Islander peoples—a not-insignificant amendment. Although it did not devolve power in any form, 1967 was neither minimalist nor conservative. The fact that the federal parliament gained express power was a major reform.

One of the rarely discussed realities post-1967 was that the same organisation of Indigenous activists who spearheaded the reform, including Faith Bandler, visited the prime minister within months of the overwhelming consensus of the Australian people with a list of suggested uses of the newly amended race power. [1] The government rejected these claims. Proving the point that significant Aboriginal developments have only come about as a consequence of Indigenous litigation and Indigenous activism, it was the tent embassy and the activism of the early seventies that motivated the Whitlam Government to use the race power to achieve land rights and other liberating reforms, most notably the enactment of the *Racial Discrimination Act.*

The suggestion that mob should agree to a symbolic/minimalist referendum in order to leverage the euphoria of a referendum win to achieve more concrete and substantive reform is ahistorical and fundamentally at odds with how political and legal systems operate. Governments are not motivated to do things out of the kindness of their hearts. There must be rules that compel them to act and institutions that keep them accountable. To dissuade Indigenous peoples of their instinct for hardheaded reform on the promise that things will be better if we defer reform is mischief.

In relation to reinventing the wheel, enough work has been committed to structural reform by Indigenous communities, parliamentary inquiries, commissions and university scholars. In regard to a settlement and addressing unfinished business, much has already been designed in terms of substance and process. Following the High Court's decision in *Mabo v Queensland (No 2)* (1992) 175 CLR 1, the federal parliament sought to negotiate a three-prong response: a statutory framework to accommodate native title claims, a land fund to compensate those people whose native title would have been extinguished, and a Social Justice

Package aimed at settling those things yet to be settled. The third prong of the Mabo settlement was never implemented. This document, developed by the Aboriginal and Torres Strait Islander Commission and the Australian Human Rights Commission's Social Justice Commissioner, had the input of Indigenous peoples around Australia. It is a good basis for a negotiated settlement. The other blueprint is the work of the Council for Aboriginal Reconciliation. Both of these resources contain an artful mix of policy, statute and constitutional amendment. Most of the suggestions for reform are common in Western and non-Western liberal democracies with Indigenous populations. [2] It is not ambitious; it is run-of-the-mill accommodation, unremarkable and sensible.

To date, the current process bears all the signs of poor process. From 2011 to 2016, the nation funded four processes in five years. Three of these processes have had no decisive response from government and the fourth is currently in train. During this period, the government created and funded a 'Vote Yes' campaign despite there being no model of reform. Having a campaign before an amendment, let alone a coherent narrative of what reform is being pursued, has made it difficult for Australians, including Indigenous communities, to have a debate. It is assumed this must be what they seek. This distinguishes the recognition project from every other referendum, including the 1967 Referendum, where the campaign was a people's movement fuelled by cups of tea, old ladies and baked cakes. And the problem the nation wanted to fix was unambiguous. The states were doing an irrefutably poor job and the federal parliament needed to have the responsibility of Indigenous people. Simple. The amendment was obvious ten years out. In fact, it was posited in the federal parliament in the 1900s. Unlike then, today there are no visible manifestations of compulsory racial segregation and a failing assimilation policy. There is a burgeoning black middle class and much integration.

Five years since the Expert Panel, the Aboriginal resistance grows stronger. Most of the mob is waiting on a model before they can say which way they would vote, a position any reasonable mind would take before forming an opinion. A number of camps exist: principled-resistance camp, resistance-to-anything camp, wait-and-see camp, and a not-yet camp. It is certain that the no-referendum option will be on the table. Driven mostly by referendum statistics, slick marketing and not a lot of constitutional law, the process has unsurprisingly stalled. The desire for the *easy* reflects many Australians' desire to want to do something, *anything.* There are many Australians of goodwill who need to be careful that, in their desire to do good, they do not end up supporting something that is paternalistic—this is what's best for you.

A STAGGERED PACKAGE OF MUTUALLY AGREED REFORM

Given the depth of the resistance and ambivalence of Aboriginal and Torres Strait Islander peoples towards 'recognition' at present, it is important to reshape the debate. This proposal is based on a decade of research and thinking on reform.

Acknowledgement of the existence of Aboriginal and Torres Strait Islander peoples and their cultures before invasion and the continuing manifestations of that culture could be committed in statutory form. This removes the community tension about which groups are recognised and which are not. A recognition Act could be passed by the Commonwealth Parliament and state and territory parliaments on the same day. This creates a 'defining moment'. It does not matter that the states already have 'recognition'.

The substance of the Act could be what Galarrwuy Yunupingu calls 'this Settlement', and should be negotiated between Indigenous peoples and the state. It should lay down the rules of respectful engagement and coexistence and addressing unfinished business.

It is important to first explain 'unfinished business'. It is here that history is a revelation and the means by which to find a way forward.

When the British arrived, the continent was occupied by Aboriginal people. At the time, empires were expanding, claiming for themselves territories not claimed by others. The legal justification was, by and large, by domestic law or the law of nations. How the British asserted sovereignty over a land is central to the unfinished business. The British, at the time of arrival, were influenced by the writings of sixteenth-century lawyer Emer de Vattel and those of Sir William Blackstone, an English jurist of the eighteenth century. Their theories of settlement, conquest and cession influenced how the British expanded and colonised countries. Put simply, Aboriginal people lived on the land when the British arrived but they did not own it in a way that the British recognised 'owned'. Thus while Aboriginal people were present, living on the land, they did not possess it in a way that the British saw as relevant. For example, Aboriginal people were not *cultivating* the land. This is why Australian historian Bill Gammage's book, *The Biggest Estate on Earth: How Aboriginals Made Australia,* is so critically acclaimed—it contests that assessment.

It mattered whether claiming a territory was done by settlement or whether by conquest and cession because each had differing implications for the reception or not of British law. Settlement occurs where the land is desert and uncultivated and it is inhabited by backward people. Conquest means that it is a forcible invasion of occupied land and cession means that there is a treaty over occupied land. In the case of conquest, the laws of people conquered apply until the Crown or other foreign power laws apply, and in regard to cession, a treaty is entered into but the Crown or foreign power abrogates it.

In regard to settlement, the settler's laws automatically apply. That is to say that if the land was uncultivated, Europeans had a right to 'bring lands into production if they were left uncultivated by the Indigenous inhabitants'. Where lands are cultivated, then they are gained through conquest or they are ceded by a treaty. Furthermore, if the land is uninhabited then the laws of the British are immediately in force, but where the lands are either conquered or ceded then the lands already have laws of their own. Until the Crown asserts sovereignty and actually changes them 'the ancient laws of the country remain'.

In the Mabo decision, the plurality argued that international law recognised conquest, cession and occupation of territory that was *terra nullius* as three of the effective ways of acquiring sovereignty, although there are competing views of what applied to Australia. In any event, the situation in Australia, in the view of the British, was that the Aboriginal people were backward people and the land was not, in their eyes, cultivated. The decision in Mabo was an uneasy combination of unsettled/settled. While it found that the land was occupied and there was a sophisticated system of laws in place, it assimilated the rules of settlement with the rules for a conquered colony to the extent of their rights and interests in land.

The unsatisfactory conquered/settled distinction has been the subject of much criticism. But this is not the fundamental issue. It is not for the courts to resolve that which the parliament must. Sovereignty was not passed from the Aboriginal people through any significant legal act. The British did not ask permission to settle. Aboriginal people did not consent and no one ceded. This is the source of disquiet. This is the grievance that must be addressed. The further we are from 1788 the less inclined the state will be to address this.

While there is a commitment to addressing the statistical disparity in health and wellbeing, employment and in education outcomes, there is a prodigious disavowal of these historical matters as relevant to health and wellbeing. Acknowledgement of the history is the foundation of *durable* solutions. 'Settlement' means to settle the matter—to agree to disagree on many facts of settlement and history and to work out a mutually agreed method of engagement in the future.

The framework for consultation and design of the agreed settlement should be time limited. The settlement agreement should be a simple text. It is a mutually agreed philosophical framework. And it should set down guidelines and principles for how the Commonwealth engages with the first nation polities across Australia in relation to policy development and design, funding, law reform and other relevant matters both parties agree to. The unimplemented, post-Mabo

Recognition, Rights and Reform report [3] is useful. It adopts a framework of institutional, structural, collaborative and co-operative reform.

It is an obvious and well-made point that there are many Aboriginal polities and therefore one overarching agreement is not appropriate. However, there are clearly fundamental principles that should underpin the engagement between the Commonwealth and Indigenous peoples. I still believe the National Aboriginal Committee's decision in 1979 to adopt the term *Makarrata* is useful. *Makarrata* is a Yolngu word from northeastern Arnhem Land that is sometimes translated as 'things are alright again after a conflict', or 'coming together after a struggle'. Most Australians would understand the sentiment. Mindful of not reinventing the wheel, the following is an extract from the post-Mabo ATSIC consultations on Principles for Indigenous Social Justice and the Development of Relations between the Commonwealth Government and Aboriginal and Torres Strait Islander Peoples:

The relationship between the Commonwealth Government and the Aboriginal and Torres Strait Islander peoples of Australia is founded in full acceptance and recognition of the fundamental rights of Aboriginal and Torres Strait Islander peoples to:

a recognition of Indigenous peoples as the original owners of this land, and of the particular rights that are associated with that status;

b the enjoyment of, and protection for, the unique, rich and diverse Indigenous cultures;

c self-determination to decide within the broad context of Australian society the priorities and the directions of their own lives, and to freely determine their own affairs;

d social justice and full equality of treatment, free from racism; and

e exercise and enjoy the full benefits and protection of international covenants. [4]

The form of the agreed principles need to be negotiated, as some of the language and aspirations may have dated. It does, however, in principle, provide an agreed path forward in terms of how multiple polities could engage with the Commonwealth, states, territories and local government. Settlement, as Patrick Dodson calls it, or 'serious business', as Galarrwuy Yunupingu describes it, can be addressed in a comprehensive package. With statutory recognition and an agreement regarding principles of future engagement and a time limit for settling other matters, the actual amendments to the Constitution should be technical in nature; for example, the race power and any other amendment that may be agreed to. The priority is amending or deleting and inserting a people's power—not a subject matter power—to make laws for Aboriginal and Torres Strait Islander peoples. This is partially in alignment with Aboriginal and Torres Strait Islander peoples' aspirations post–*Kartinyeri v Commonwealth* (1998) 195 CLR 337.

A racial non-discrimination clause or a voice in the parliament are both important constitutional reforms. In fact, there is less pressure on the drafting of a new or amended 'people's power' if there is a racial non-discrimination clause. In the absence of this clause the debate about the race power becomes more complicated. Either way, polling has shown both clauses would have the support of many sectors of the Australian community.

Finally, we must as Australians become used to describing reconciliation as a process, not a destination. A settlement is a living document. The post–Mabo settlement consultations found that Aboriginal and Torres Strait Islander peoples wanted a document to be 'capable of accommodating change and evolution as both Indigenous and non-Indigenous cultures change and evolve'. Communities sensibly acknowledged that 'a document in itself will not overcome the historical injustices which have been the lot of Indigenous peoples' [5] but that the recognition of fundamental principles of engagement and a process for resolving other matters is a useful, productive and collaborative starting point.

LISTEN AND REFORM

The fact that no one *hears* what it is that Aboriginal people are saying has been a cause of despair; it is why the gap in inequality is not closing, and it highlights the exigency of reform. If the state were to hear what it is Aboriginal and Torres Strait Islander peoples are saying, then we could agree to address the unresolved historical issues that continue to inform contemporary issues. In the meantime, the passage from the Henry Wadsworth Longfellow poem is worth citing in full because it so acutely and incisively captures what is a seemingly irresolvable tension between the settler and the colonised:

> Ships that pass in the night, and speak each other in passing, Only a signal shown and a distant voice in the darkness; *So on the ocean of life we pass and speak one another,* Only a look and a voice, then darkness again and a silence.

8

BUILDING A NEW, BETTER LEGACY

Kirstie Parker

> We cringe like dogs at the prospect of the 'White backlash'. We pray eternally that the White authority structure will not turn on us and impede what little progress we have made. We ask for land rights with tongue in cheek, knowing full well in our hearts that the land belonged to us in the first instance. We stagger and stumble into each other in confusion when our identity ... is contested and thus allow ourselves to be moulded by others. Our land, our pride and our future has been taken away from us and our people buried in unmarked graves. We wander through Australian society as beggars. We live off the crumbs of the white Australian table and are told to be grateful... [1]

So the late dr Charles Perkins AO once opined and, many years later, arguably barely more sadly prescient words could be spoken about the situation that we now find ourselves in.

It is 2016 and the nation is grappling with how it might reform its founding document to recognise Aboriginal and Torres Strait Islander peoples as the first peoples of this cherished place. Yet, like a child who has never been in a kitchen expected to bake themselves a tasty birthday cake to the liking of everyone else but them, here we are. If that and the rest of this chapter seem a bit impolite, so be it. Australians generally pride themselves on calling a spade a spade. Here, now, we must.

A touchstone in this current process is what is frequently referred to as the 1967 Referendum, held on 27 May in that year, when more than 90 per cent of the nation voted 'Yes' to give federal parliament the power to make laws in relation to Aboriginal and Torres Strait Islander peoples and to include us in the national census.

Notwithstanding the generally revered place of that historic event, it has evoked differing and shifting views among our people. Some, like the late author and activist Burnum Burnum, felt it made a powerful difference, declaring, 'At the time, I definitely thought that the referendum achieved something—personally it made me lose my inferiority complex. It also made me prouder to proclaim my Aboriginality' [2], while others, like the late playwright and activist Kevin Gilbert, demurred, telling a gathering at the Aboriginal Tent Embassy in Canberra on the 25th anniversary in 1992, 'If the Referendum hadn't been passed, we would have been further advanced because white

Australia would not have fooled the world into thinking that something positive was being done.' [3]

Fast forward and some, like former Prime Minister Tony Abbott, have ventured more recently that the 50th anniversary of the 1967 Referendum—on 27 May 2017—would be a nice date for us to settle this thing.

And wouldn't it just, in a perfect world?

But, aside from the potential for a future failed referendum to sully the memory of what was a watershed moment in Australia's history, I believe we still have a long road to travel before we can know for sure that we should proceed to a new referendum at all, let alone when.

Let it not be lost on any of us that the day before 27 May is National Sorry Day, which acknowledges the experiences of tens of thousands of Aboriginal and Torres Strait Islander children forcibly removed from their families under government policies and practices—an act of extreme violence against us and one from which, still today, we have scarcely begun to recover.

While in recovery mode, we are also very much still in the middle of ongoing assault on our existence, our connection to country and our cultures—our human rights. What does it say that:

- we can expect to live ten to seventeen years less than other Australians, and experience higher rates of preventable illness such as heart disease, kidney disease and diabetes as well as mental illness;

- babies born to our mothers die at more than twice the rate of other Australian babies;
- the number of our children separated from family and community is at record highs, much higher now than during what is referred to as the Stolen Generations era;
- we're just 3 per cent of the broader Australian population but make up 27 per cent of the prison population, generally (and 34 per cent for our women);
- nationally, our men are twice as likely to be in prison than in university;
- our women are hospitalised due to family violence–related assaults at a rate 34.2 times that for non-Indigenous females;
- our unemployment rate is at least four times that of the general population;
- despite recognition of native title and various state and territory land rights regimes, most of our communities are still impoverished and glean very little economic benefit from what is ours;
- punitive, shaming measures, such as income management, can be imposed disproportionately on our people;

- our remote communities can be threatened with closure because it is apparently too expensive to countenance delivering to them the essential services that most Australians take for granted;
- vital community-controlled health, legal, childcare and other services can be drip-fed funding via chaotic grant processes, and others cut off entirely;
- our current and still fledgling elected representative body, the National Congress of Australia's First Peoples (congress), has been defunded and largely ignored in favour of a non-elected advisory council handpicked by government;
- we live in a country that repeatedly puts its hand on its heart and pledges internationally to respect our human rights and honour the standards enshrined in the *UN Declaration on the Rights of Indigenous Peoples* and a range of other international instruments but does nothing of the sort;
- the annual celebration of our national identity takes place on the anniversary of an event that still tears viciously at Aboriginal and Torres Strait Islander peoples' memory, and any requests to reconsider the date are met with howls of 'get over it'?

This is all in the context where we are being asked to contemplate reform of the Australian Constitution. The questions, 'How can we trust our hearts with governments that have presided over, and indeed propelled us towards our current perilous circumstances?' and 'Is government even competent enough for us to engage with?' ring loudly in our ears.

Constitutional reform is more than a fascinating legal conundrum; it's about our lives and they matter.

OUR VOICE

For me, the current government's lack of support for and engagement with congress speaks volumes. It has been gravely insulting to the very concept of a voice 'chosen by our people, for our people'. It also flies in the face of Australia's endorsement of the UN's declaration, which enshrines Indigenous peoples' rights to maintain and develop their own decision-making institutions, as well as the commitment of UN states to consult and co-operate in good faith with such institutions and provide the financial and technical assistance needed to enable the enjoyment of all rights contained in the declaration.

Even in its still evolving state, congress is regarded within the UN system as a central mechanism for government to negotiate with on the rights of our people. The former and current prime ministers both said they valued and would meet with this representative body, which counts among its number more than 8500 individuals and around 180 organisations, including virtually all of the national peak bodies. Former Prime Minister Abbott never did and, six months after taking office, Prime Minister

Malcolm Turnbull has yet to. The clock continues to tick.

WHOSE PSYCHE?

It has been suggested that a 'successful' referendum on this matter would 'complete' the nation, and an unsuccessful one would be catastrophic for the national psyche and ongoing process of reconciliation, not to mention embarrassing for Australia on the international stage. But that is not especially persuasive among an audience who live catastrophe virtually every day. What of the Aboriginal and Torres Strait Islander peoples' psyche? Is it any wonder that the whispering in the most optimistic and hopeful of black hearts grows more strident every day?

Today, we live with imperfect outcomes of the 1967 Referendum; perpetually underwhelming outcomes from native title and the broader response to the historic High Court decision in *Mabo v Queensland (No 2)* (1992) 175 CLR 1; lingering pain from the Stolen Generations despite the National Apology in 2008; achingly slow progress in closing health, life expectancy, education, employment and other gaps; and no serious governmental commitment to addressing burning issues, like over-incarceration. With so many hopes raised and dashed, so many promises made and broken, so much optimism squandered, it is no surprise that we are fatigued and flagging. Still, we are told to be patient and not to knock too hard on the door.

While his predecessor professed and, some would say, demonstrated a deep personal commitment to the issue of constitutional change, it remains to be seen if Prime Minister Turnbull will match and better it in real terms.

It is a telling and serious indictment on successive governments that, after five years of committees and recommendations on the subject (and the prospect of more still with the work of the new Referendum Council), Australia still does not have a proposal to consider. So far, we've had little from government and constitutional conservatives—so-called 'Con-cons'—other than pre-emptive undermining of particular measures, including the Expert Panel on the Recognition of Aboriginal and Torres Strait Islander Peoples' recommendation of a non-discrimination provision and Noel Pearson's pitch for a constitutionally enshrined Indigenous body to advise government, combatted by some principled pushback from the Labor Opposition. But understand this: any reform of the Constitution must involve substantive change and lay the foundation for the fair treatment of our peoples. And we must have the final say on any referendum about us.

This was the clear message from a group of Aboriginal and Torres Strait Islander people, including myself and my then fellow congress co-chair, Les Malezer, who met in July last year with then Prime Minister Abbott and the Opposition Leader Bill Shorten, to map a way forward on constitutional reform. The make-up of that group remains contentious within our communities but, apart from saying that it was determined by the PM's office and kept from us right up until the moment we walked into the room at Kirribilli, that issue will be left for another time. But it irks me that we subsequently had to cajole and fight so hard to secure an Aboriginal and Torres Strait Islander designed and led process of consultation—dubbed 'the black process'—to gauge our views and level of support for the various proposals that have emerged over time.

What is shaping up to be a series of regional gatherings, culminating in a national Aboriginal and Torres Strait Islander convention, is a no-brainer and should have been undertaken long before now. It will constitute a significant amount of heavy lifting in this so-far flawed process and, I believe, has helped to stem growing cynicism within our community ... for now.

And so here we are.

WHAT THEN?

Through my previous shared stewardship of congress, I am on the record as supporting the recommendations of the Expert Panel following what remains the most exhaustive contemporary consultation process on constitutional reform, and my position has not changed. I continue to support reform that would ensure recognition of us as the first peoples of Australia, preserve the Commonwealth's power to make laws with respect to us, and, in making laws under such a power, prevent the Commonwealth from discriminating against us. If Noel Pearson's suggestion of a constitutionally enshrined body was to come to pass, I believe that body's membership should be determined wholly by us and it should have as much 'grunt' as possible in terms of compelling the government and the broader parliament to take notice.

Beyond this, I feel no pressure to alone micro design the inspired raft of measures warranted, extending beyond just reform of the Constitution to, potentially, legislation, a treaty/treaties, and genuine implementation of the UN's declaration. That is the purpose of the black process and, subject to and after that, consideration by the parliament and ultimately the Australian people.

OPTIMISTIC STILL

In challenging times like this, I look to our families, communities, organisations and achievements for emotional sustenance.

My late grandfather toiled in the paddock and shearing shed from sunrise to sundown for little more than mutton, flour, sugar, tea and tobacco; my late mum started work as a domestic servant from the age of eleven and went on to study at university and run two businesses. They and many others stood up for our current and future generations, and I'm determined that their efforts will not have been in vain.

Despite the ongoing legacy of history, fatigue around constitutional reform and the fact that it is not us but the non-Indigenous majority who will determine the outcome of any referendum, we are still mighty, nurtured by country and culture, and the knowledge that there are many good people—women and men—standing with us. I revel in the staunch camaraderie of decent non-Indigenous Australians in efforts such as the national Close the Gap and Change the Record campaigns.

I believe that together we can, yet, build a new legacy—a better one where all who walk this land are happy, healthy and have their human rights respected. And where the relationship between us is healed, in truth and genuine reconciliation. I yearn for that but it will depend on how courageous we are, collectively, now and going forward.

Real reform, not mere change, is the end goal here. That's what is worth fighting for and, with skilful and respectful handling, even the hardest or most closed of hearts are capable of softening and opening. Just don't tell us that it doesn't matter how we're recognised, just that we are. That would take the cake.

9

CONSTITUTIONAL RECOGNITION: A CASE FOR LESS IS MORE

Asmi Wood

History has shown that achieving complex constitutional change in Australia is difficult. The double-majority hurdle required to effect constitutional change means that majority perspectives will determine the final outcome of any particular referendum. On the other hand, the impact of any future referendum on the recognition of Aboriginal and Torres Strait Islander peoples in the Constitution will primarily impact the Indigenous community. It would be natural and reasonable, therefore, that Indigenous people would ideally like maximal 'positive' change, including the urgent need to reverse the legal fictions responsible for the injustices of the past, and to do so at the next referendum.

Voters, often guided by their leaders and against their better judgement, generally are sceptical of expanding 'powers' or 'rights', particularly constitutional change, the impact of which they do not fully understand.

Therefore, the majority swayed by the leaders will almost certainly be likely to favour symbolism over substantial change. Failure to garner majority support means that the status quo remains, and a rare opportunity to improve the law may be wasted, depending on the form of recognition. Bearing that in mind, any future referendum should *only* be seen as an opportunity to take the nation forward a single step in the proverbial thousand-mile journey towards fully rectifying the wrongs of the past, not as a just outcome but as perhaps a possible practical outcome.

Ideally, and even in practice, many people would say contemporary 'Australian values' could easily accommodate notions of Aboriginal equality in a fuller sense—encouraging Aboriginal languages, celebrating Aboriginal culture as a whole, valuing Aboriginal history and historical sites, engendering sharing, and celebrating Aboriginal ways as the longest continuous living culture—and that this would be welcomed by most Australians but for the fearmongering of the vociferous few. Consequently, and unfortunately, we must avoid the understandable temptation of attempting to rectify all past wrongs, while simultaneously entrenching positive provisions for the future, all in one fell swoop. The historical verity of wrongs perpetrated against Indigenous peoples is considered self-evident.

History shows that the voting public appear to be more amenable to rescinding offensive parts of the Constitution that do not fit in with their contemporary mores, than they are to accede to complex new provisions or text, especially those which do not find clear multi-party support. Unlike the current situation, the 1967 Referendum had the universal support of the Indigenous community and was a case in point where the vast majority of Australians did support what they thought were changes to herald in a new acceptance of Indigenous people as equal partners in the broader community, and to do so by rescinding parts of the Constitution.

The more complex the proposed changes, the less predictable their legal effect, thus possibly increasing the risk of failure at the ballot box. On the other hand, perhaps the only thing worse than not gaining positive change is to further entrench harmful provisions. To this end, possible changes to the Constitution that are simple have predictable results, which are more positive than negative—for the majority of Australians, anyway—and which are likely to gain majority support.

WHAT DO 'INDIGENOUS PEOPLE' WANT?

The first question is determining what it is that Indigenous people want from the referendum. There are likely to be a range of answers to this question. Thus, any attempted comprehensive answer is likely to be flawed, speculative, essentialist or simply wrong. However, even an approximation of an answer would help establish a relative yardstick to which other proposals can be compared. But it is conceded that a significant minority of Indigenous people would like to disengage from the process.

A longer-term answer to the question raised above, expressed as a broad general statement that might be reasonably representative, is that Indigenous people would like to be in a position post-referendum that would have *evolved* or improved. Perhaps, in the current context, a vision of domestic sovereignty as articulated by many Indigenous lawyers and thinkers, including Tony McAvoy SC and Michael Mansell, is an approximation of what is ideal.

Alternatively, one may attempt to glean an answer to the question, 'but for' colonisation, in what position would Indigenous people otherwise likely to have been? The answer, though, is likely to be a rough, not-entirely-satisfactory approximation only. A reply to the 'but for' question may be that Indigenous cultures would have organically evolved over the two centuries, and that many languages and much law and culture would have been adapted, but largely maintained relatively intact, though subjected to external influences such as the United Nations, the treaty systems and the general effect of norm-setting in international and regional organisations. Even if this evolved position could be described accurately, and were to be embraced by Australians as what Indigenous people want from the referendum, at present, the political will required to deliver 'ideal change' is absent, as evidenced by the slow uptake of the considered proposals resulting from broad consultation with the Australian people by the Expert Panel on Constitutional Recognition of Aboriginal and Torres Strait Islander Peoples and the Joint Select Committee.

Thus, an amendment that is likely to pass at a referendum needs to be confined to those parameters and political will. A unique feature of the settler–colonial society is that Indigenous aspirations for change, unless very modest and constrained, are unlikely to be supported. The arduous process of change is compounded by the entrenched inertia of the present Constitution and a fearful constituency, one that is still to come to terms with its own history.

Thus the thousand-mile journey has to be accomplished in small, considered steps over a longer period of time. This is because of the significant gap that exists between an ideal and the reality, which has resulted from over two hundred years of colonisation. This gap is, unfortunately, unlikely to be breached in our lifetimes, although hopefully within our grandchildren's lifetimes. Consequently, a non-negotiable precondition for the longer term must also envisage that Indigenous cultures, languages and laws should be maintained and fostered, through measures that can be adopted under the present law, so that significant 'reconnection' to law and culture by our grandchildren somewhere down the thousand-mile road is possible. This perhaps slightly pessimistic view should be tempered by the fact that Indigenous people and cultures have survived arguably the harshest and most coercive assimilationist periods in their history. The question, however, remains as to whether Indigenous people and culture can resist the seductive lure of a consumerist culture and the uniform homogenising mundaneness of universal materialism—an entirely separate issue faced by many cultures, and an issue outside the scope of this essay.

'Recognition', subject to its form, is a pre-condition for longer-term solutions. Parties cannot enter into a treaty or conclude negotiations on issues such as sovereignty unless they legally recognise the other. That is, legal personality is a crucial prerequisite for establishing legal relations, and recognition will translate *de facto* recognition (as recognised as true by many) into a *de lege* fact, entrenched in the nation's *grundnorm.* To that end, it really does matter whether Indigenous peoples agree to or consent to this reform.

On the other hand, as the leader of the opposition Bill Shorten said, symbolic recognition alone, without more, would be 'empty poetry' because constitutional recognition is primarily about making Anglo-Australian law internally consistent. Symbolic recognition alone would still leave a Constitution that treats Indigenous people as second-class citizens through their vulnerability to constitutionally sanctioned discrimination, whether or not such treatment is characterised as 'beneficial', a reactionary power that should be rescinded in a post-apartheid world.

GETTING TO CHANGE

The Constitution prescribes the mode by which it may be changed, which is that a majority of people in the majority of the states must vote in favour of a proposition. This necessarily means that it is not the 2.2 per cent of Indigenous people who will decide what changes, if any, will be adopted. Indigenous people are not, however, voiceless or powerless, as many in the majority will take heed of Indigenous opinions. While consensus is more easily imagined than achieved in practice, consensus would provide Indigenous people with the purchase they need to urge and encourage change in a particular direction.

In 2010, Prime Minister Julia Gillard appointed the Expert Panel, including recognised Indigenous legal experts, to examine Indigenous recognition and its related issues. The Expert Panel conducted extensive consultations with the general Australian public and produced an excellent, comprehensive and readable report, which is mandatory reading for those interested in this referendum. In examining the question of recognition, the Expert Panel also noted the public's aversion to tokenism as well as a strong desire to recognise the historical wrongs and to treat Indigenous people decently in the future, flagging the possibilities for change.

The Expert Panel canvassed several possible options for change, respectfully considered a wide variety of views and fairly sought to give effect, as best they could within its tightly circumscribed terms of reference, to the large number of competing but relevant considerations, opinions and aspirations of both Indigenous and non-Indigenous people. The parliament subsequently entrusted to the Joint Select Committee the task of adapting the Expert Panel's recommendations for a referendum. I respectfully suggest that they have not been able to achieve this. In effect, the Expert Panel's report still remains the more useful resource for this purpose.

An important factor in favour of constitutional recognition of Indigenous people, and thus entrenched Indigenous legal personality, is that Australian common law has already evolved from the point of denying the existence of Indigenous people *(terra nullius)* at the time of colonisation, to excluding them from the count of the human population at Federation (in section 117), to a gradual recognition of their civilisations (perhaps first articulated in the law by his Honour Justice Blackburn in the Supreme Court of the Northern Territory). Since then the common law has recognised that Australia had an Indigenous population who possessed rights and interests acquired under their own normative systems (in *Mabo v Queensland (No 2)* (1992) 175 CLR 1).

The Australian Constitution, its *grundnorm* or basis, however, remains deficient in this respect, as it remains unchanged from when first promulgated at Federation, when it denied the existence of an Indigenous human population on the continent. Many people would like to rectify this situation, which is wrong and embarrassing for a modern liberal democracy that otherwise has a wonderful record in many fields of human endeavour.

Further, and as recognised by the Expert Panel, a desire to treat Indigenous people equally was demonstrated by the public in 1967 and has been since. Unfortunately, as shown some years later by the High Court, the legal changes effected at that referendum did not fully translate the aspirations and sentiments of equal beneficial treatment into law. At the next referendum, Australia has the opportunity to complete this unfinished business.

The Expert Panel and the subsequent parliamentary reports have formulated words of recognition that could be included in the Constitution. The statement of recognition as suggested by the Expert Panel and others could, in their opinion, reasonably have some legal effect. Therefore, their choice of words have been somewhat muted. I propose that recognition, on which rights or obligations are *not* contingent, will allow the use of generous, poetic language—also a more accurate depiction of Indigenous custodianship, and their love, connection and care for the land. The legal importance of this symbolic step then is to make Anglo-Australian law internally consistent, synchronising its Constitution and law, while concurrently entrenching Indigenous legal personality.

A primary advantage of symbolic recognition is that because no rights or obligations will attach, they will not be contingent on a finding of an individual's indigeneity. Importantly, this will negate the need for determinations of a person's identity, which, in the circumstances, will primarily be made by non-Indigenous decision-makers and are likely to be offensive to many Indigenous people in ceding this fundamental aspect of 'self' to the bureaucracy or judiciary, if rights were recognised.

Mere constitutional recognition is too modest an aspiration for what Prime Minister Malcolm Turnbull referred to as a twenty-first century government when he took office in September 2015. As noted, Australian voters generally are reluctant to change the Constitution. On the other hand, removing text from the Constitution, particularly when the resultant changes are in keeping with majority mores, appears much more achievable. Thus in 1967, the rescission of a provision mandating the constitutional bar against counting Indigenous people in the census, a change that was both politically significant and legally substantial, was one such example. For a government of a modern industrial country, with an eye firmly to the future, it is vital to bring its nineteenth-century Constitution into the twenty-first century. Expunging the word and notion of race from the Constitution is a clearly feasible, practical and simple exercise, which is very likely to be supported by the vast majority of voters.

There are currently two remaining race provisions in the Constitution. The first is section 25, which deals with the consequences for states if they disqualify a particular race from voting in state elections. The rescission of section 25 has wide support. The second, more insidious provision is section 51(xxvi)—the so-called 'races power'—which originally provided for the regulation of 'coloured and inferior' races 'other than aboriginal natives'. In 1967 this provision was amended to extend the parliament's power to also make laws for Indigenous people ('aboriginal natives' in constitutional language). The constitutional power of section 51(xxvi) permits parliament to make 'special laws' for a people of a race, a notion based on the debunked 'scientific' concept from the time of the founding fathers for whom the 'science' of eugenics was real. Race is now predominantly accepted as socially constructed with no objective biological measure.

Section 51(xxvi) has only been used for the regulation of the Indigenous minority, including protection of cultural heritage, native title laws and the suite of laws enabling the Northern Territory Intervention. These are generally considered by many to be detrimental to Indigenous people and, if there was any doubt, the suspension of the *Racial Discrimination Act 1975* (Cth) was deemed necessary. Further, Solicitor-General Gavin Griffith QC admitted to the

High Court in the *Kartinyeri v Commonwealth (1998)* case (also known as the Hindmarsh Island bridge affair) that this constitutional power could permit the enactment of Nazi-like laws, hardly a ringing endorsement for its retention. It is inconceivable that race-based laws can be justified as a pretext for addressing Indigenous detriment. Thus, denying parliament the constitutional power to make racist laws is vital for Australia, a country that advocates for the protection of human rights and dignity on the international plane.

The founding fathers clearly saw the need for altering the Constitution in time and provided a mechanism, albeit a very stringent and difficult means, by which it could be changed by the people. Constitutional interpretation, if performed within the standard socalled 'originalist' and 'positivist' approach, in addition to the literal text of a provision, will likely give some weight to the intentions of the founders for the inclusion of that particular provision. The founders' inclusion of a race power was to prevent the inclusion of an equality clause and explicitly permitting the making of laws to discriminate against 'coloured and inferior' races but, as mentioned, left the regulation of the 'aboriginal natives' to the states.

In determining the legal effect of the 1967 changes, the majority of the High Court rejected the notion that the effected changes prevented the parliament from making detrimental laws for Indigenous peoples. Perhaps the rescission of remaining race provisions is likely to mean that the High Court prospectively will not permit the making of specific race-based laws, although the enactment of laws of general application that have a practical impact on a particular group of people or race arguably remains possible. Further, while race will cease to be a useable head of power within the Constitution, 'race', as both a legal and social construct, is still likely to remain within the law and the jurisprudence for some time to come. How a successful rescission of race from the Constitution will play out for the treatment of Indigenous people in the future will remain to be seen.

In the *Leeth v Commonwealth (1992)* case in the High Court, the Honourable Justices William Deane and Mary Gaudron, in the minority, suggested the existence of an implied right of equality in the Constitution. The majority in that case dismissed this notion. The mere existence of the races power clearly means that the minority position is not supportable, but it certainly indicates the High Court's willingness to contemplate the existence of an implied right, if the conditions in the future are right. While an implied right is clearly weaker than the strong, positive anti-discrimination provision as proposed by the Expert Panel, former Prime Minister Tony Abbott rejected this provision as a 'one clause bill of rights', a statement that has not been contradicted by his party, thus suggesting that it will not be supported at a referendum.

It is posited that the rescission of the races power from the Constitution would then allow the High Court to discover the existence of an implied right to racial equality in the Constitution for all Australian citizens, entrenching the common law notion of a right to equality before the law. (The 'aliens' power will still allow parliament to make detrimental laws for aliens.) In any event, the absence of the races power will ensure that parliament will find it difficult to make racist laws in future. Beneficial laws may still be enacted under sections of the Racial Discrimination Act, although a specific examination of this issue is outside the scope of this chapter.

A PROPOSED QUESTION FOR THE NEXT REFERENDUM?

What we need is the inclusion of a generous statement of recognition, entrenching Indigenous legal personality without legal consequence and making it unnecessary for others to determine Indigenous identity for the purposes of the law. The rescission of the races provisions, thus preventing future parliaments from making laws with respect to Indigenous people only, is also necessary. This does not, as some people imply, remove parliament's power to rectify disadvantage through laws of general application. The current common law as codified in the Native Title Act permits the recognition of rights and obligations that inhere in the pre-colonial legal traditions, and entrenchment will ensure that this will continue into the future.

The Expert Panel and others have clearly articulated the wish of the vast majority of voters to end race-based discrimination. The rescission of the races power will allow this to become a reality with respect to race. It is therefore proposed that a referendum question, such as 'Do you support the rescission of the race provisions from the Constitution and require parliament to presume and treat all citizens equally before the law?', is likely to get a resounding 'Yes' vote and allow all Australians to hold their heads up with dignity by bringing their Constitution into the twenty-first century, a further step along the thousand-mile journey.

10

A PLACE AT THE CONSTITUTIONAL TABLE

Nolan Hunter

As indigenous people, and as human beings, we have rights to self-determination. Self-determination means the right to freely pursue social, economic and cultural development. This is the most basic of all the human rights—and one our 'Freedom Commissioner' in particular should well understand.

The right to self-determination is protected by Article 3 of the *United Nations Declaration on the Rights of Indigenous Peoples,* and other human rights instruments. In a practical sense, self-determination means that our people should be the primary decision-makers in our own lives, and in the lives of our communities. We should not have decisions made about us without our genuine input.

Do we want to allow economic development on our land, or preserve it for environmental and cultural purposes? That should be our choice.

Do we have ideas about making our remote communities sustainable, or should they be closed?

We should be able to negotiate to this effect, and to put forward our own ideas for our futures.

> In short, we should have a place at the table. Article 18 of the UN declaration states:
>
> Indigenous peoples have the right to participate in decisionmaking in matters which would affect their rights, through representatives chosen by themselves in accordance with their own procedures, as well as to maintain and develop their own Indigenous decision-making institutions.

Article 19 states:

> States shall consult and cooperate in good faith with the Indigenous peoples concerned through their own representative institutions in order to obtain their free, prior and informed consent before adopting and implementing legislative or administrative measures that may affect them.

Australia has in many respects failed to implement the principles of the UN declaration. There are no structures for Indigenous participation and consultation to happen fairly. Decisions are generally made about us without our input.

Recently we were in New York, appealing to the United Nations in this regard. Our anxiety was over the forced closure of Indigenous communities. This decision was yet again made without consultation. The Western

Australia premier now says that he will consult before any further decisions are made. This is at least a step in the right direction. But what did our people have to do to achieve this change in attitude? We became protesters, as we always do, resorting to rallies, resorting to the United Nations.

Where is our formal place at the table in our own nation? Where is our negotiation table with government—our space for measured and rational debate and conversation? For nuanced policy discussion? Why do we have to go to New York before someone will listen to us?

The time has come for Australia to implement the essential principles of the UN declaration, and put formal structures in place for us to always have a say in the political decisions and laws that are made about us.

Other countries are way ahead. New Zealand has the Treaty of Waitangi, reserved Maori seats in parliament, as well as the Maori Council—a national representative body for Maori to have a voice in their affairs. They have the Waitangi Tribunal for Maori tribes to negotiate and make settlements with the Crown. In the United Nations, we see how far ahead many other nations are in ensuring representation and recognition of their indigenous people. Norway and Sweden have Sami parliaments to advise government on the issues of the Sami people.

When will Australia guarantee Indigenous Australians a voice in our own affairs? Other Western nations like Canada and the United States have full bills of rights in their constitutions. But bills of rights are not the only way to protect human rights. Participation and consultation is another way to do it.

Too often, human rights lawyers here are stuck in their bill of rights bubble. They pursue constitutional rights clauses, whether or not bipartisan support can be achieved for that kind of reform. Bills of rights engage courts and judges: more non-Indigenous people, usually, deciding what is good for us. Our people have fought enough court battles to know this is true. Bills of rights and court battles are necessary and important. But they are not the only way forward.

What about having a place at the political table?

Father Frank Brennan keeps using that phrase, but does he know what it means? Has he thought about how a place at the table might be achieved for our people, in a way that is authoritative and enduring?

We are the ones who live every day in our communities, struggling towards a better future, struggling for our rights to live as equals in Australia. Struggling to be heard. Perhaps the lawyers don't understand this. For us, our voicelessness is real.

Noel Pearson's proposal for an Indigenous consultative and representative body in the Constitution is the only proposal that could implement both Indigenous people's rights to be properly consulted where government laws affect our interests, and the right of Indigenous people to participate, through our own institutions, in the political decision-making that affects us.

Constitutional recognition should guarantee us a place at the table. After all, the government has a special power to legislate for us. If a referendum happens, they will have a specific Indigenous power to make laws about us.

If we do not fight for this proposal, we will still be in the powerless position we are in now, even after a referendum happens. The government will have its Indigenous power, but we will still have no say in the laws that it makes under that power. That would be a poor outcome, and is not a reform worth fighting for.

Our people need to see the opportunity that is before us. This is about achieving a successful referendum for something meaningful that will actually make a difference in our lives. The Constitution should respect our human rights and our rights as Indigenous people. But 'human rights' does not mean just one thing. It does not only mean bills of rights.

It also means self-determination. The right to choose our own destinies. It means participation and consultation. Our human rights can also be protected through proper processes and procedures. By guaranteeing us a say in our affairs. By negotiating fairly when decisions are made.

We hope that our fellow Indigenous leaders will see this for the important opportunity it is. Our people have a right to a place at the table and a say in the laws that are made about us. It is this right that deserves constitutional recognition.

11

REFUGEES IN OUR OWN COUNTRY

Dawn Casey

Buoyed by the whitlam Government's transformative legislative reforms, particularly the *Racial Discrimination Act 1975* (Cth) and the development of the Northern Territory Land Rights Bill subsequently enacted by Prime Minister Malcolm Fraser's conservative government, our first nations peoples were optimistic of furthering the pursuit of recognition and self-determination into the 1980s. The momentum at the time was not dissimilar to the decade prior to the 1967 Referendum. The outcomes our Indigenous peoples were seeking were aligned: recognition through national land rights, a treaty and formal structures that would ensure Indigenous peoples had direct access to government and the leadership in the development and implementation of policies and programs. The views on how this was to be achieved did vary, and in some cases varied dramatically!

CAPRICIOUSNESS OF POLITICS CONTINUES THE DISPOSSESSION

The widely held descriptions of the 1980s being the decade of boom and bust hold true also for Indigenous affairs. The state of mind of our first nations peoples went from one of elation to feelings of utter betrayal by the Labor Government.

Prime Minister Bob Hawke's commitment to negotiate a treaty was reduced to a process of reconciliation and national land rights legislation was abandoned. The Labor Government did, however, enact legislation that went a long way towards self-determination in the form of the Aboriginal and Torres Strait Islander Commission (ATSIC).

In 2003, just thirteen years after it took effect, the Howard Government with the support of a Labor led by Mark Latham agreed ATSIC had not worked and it was formally abolished at midnight on 24 March 2005. Labor subsequently established the National Congress of Australia's First Peoples as a public company with members being elected by Indigenous peoples. Upon coming to power, the Abbott Government defunded the congress and selected a range of Indigenous people and others from the wider Australian community to advise it on Indigenous policies and programs.

Running parallel to the pursuit of self-determination and land rights within the spheres of government, John Koowarta from the Wik nation and Eddie Koiki Mabo and four Meriam people from the Torres Strait island of Mer took their fights to the courts in the late 1970s and 1980s. The High Court's decision in relation to Koowarta upheld the validity of Australia's Racial Discrimination Act.

Having lost his battle to have the Commonwealth's Racial Discrimination Act declared invalid, then Queensland Premier Joh Bjelke-Petersen used the power of his government with all of its might to prevent John Koowarta from acquiring the lease of the Archer River pastoral property by converting the pastoral lease into a national park.

In 1992, the High Court decided in *Mabo v Queensland (No 2)* (1992) 175 CLR 1 that customary law native title could be recognised by common law, reversing the longstanding doctrine of *terra nullius*—that the land of Australia had belonged to no one when the British arrived. For the first time in the history of the colonisation of Australia, our first nations peoples had a foundation from which to negotiate with governments.

At the time, the mood was palpable and reverberated through governments, industries and the media alike nationally. Prime Minister Paul Keating negotiated unsuccessfully with the state governments and the mining industry for several months for a response to the decision prior to his announcement of the establishment of the Mabo Unit within the Department of Prime Minister and Cabinet to consult with the Indigenous community.

The *Native Title Act 1993* was the central part of the national settlement, providing a means to have native title determined as well as other processes.

As part of the complex negotiations to put in place a statutory framework for native title, the Indigenous leaders agreed to the validation of government Acts to extinguish native title between 1975, when the Racial Discrimination Act came into force, and the date of the Native Title Act. This meant land title certainty for other Australians.

Many Indigenous Australians were unlikely to benefit from the Native Title Act because their traditional land had already been alienated. So the Land Account—then called the Land Fund—was legislated to provide some compensation for the widespread dispossession of Indigenous peoples since 1788. Neither Labor nor conservative governments have delivered on the third part of the agreed settlement, the Native Title Social Justice Package.

There have been a series of amendments to the original Native Title Act, including and most particularly Prime Minister John Howard's harsh response to the High Court's Wik decision in 1996.

As with any legislation, the Native Title Act has not lived up to the expectations of some of our people. For others, however, the Act has provided access to land and resources, and a right to negotiate about the future of land that is, or may be, subject to native title.

Another outcome of the Mabo judgement was the establishment of the Indigenous Land Corporation (ILC). The ILC has unique independence from government. The corporation has its own source of revenue, the Land Account, the compensatory fund legislated as part of the 'Grand Bargain'. Its board has a majority of Indigenous directors. They are appointed by the Indigenous Affairs Minister but cannot be directed by the minister. The ILC currently has the discretion and flexibility to pursue Indigenous benefits over the longer term, at arm's length from political or budgetary cycles.

Just a couple of months after the election of the Abbott Government in September 2013, the Minister for Indigenous Affairs initiated a review of the ILC and Indigenous Business Australia (IBA). There can be little doubt that Senator Nigel Scullion's view was that the ILC and IBA should be merged. As Opposition Spokesperson on Indigenous Affairs, he was quoted in the media in relation to the appointment of the ILC CEO: 'The [then] Minister,' he said, 'was appointing someone to a position that might not exist after the election.'

One of the terms of reference for the ILC/IBA review had asked the reviewers to consider 'appropriate powers of Ministerial direction or Government control'. The ILC board saw the ILC/IBA review as a serious threat to a basic part of the native title settlement: the Aboriginal and Torres Strait Islander Land Account now worth $2 billion. In a merged agency, the Land Account's revenues would inevitably be used, sooner or later, for purposes other than those originally legislated.

The government's own reviewers, the accounting firm Ernst & Young, found that both the ILC and IBA are operating well. They recommended some reorientation of effort, but considered that the two agencies should remain as stand-alone entities, given their different histories and purposes.

The ILC's principal strategy in the face of this threat was to develop a draft bill to amend the governing legislation, the *Aboriginal and Torres Strait Islander Act 2005.* The draft of the Stronger Land Account Bill was released in March 2014, and endorsed on the same day by a group of senior Indigenous leaders, including three who had helped to negotiate the Mabo settlement and served on the first ILC board. The draft bill also addressed the serious shortcomings in governance practices identified in the Deloitte Review of Board Corporate Governance and the McGrathNicol Acquisition Ayers Rock Resort.

The key amendments proposed by the Stronger Land Account Bill are as follows:

- It seeks to protect and strengthen the Land Account by making the Land Account's purpose specify that the Land Account is a compensatory mechanism in acknowledgement of past injustices and dispossession of traditional lands and acknowledging the special relationship Aboriginal and Torres Strait Islanders have with their lands.
- It seeks to ensure that funds from the Land Account can be used only for land-related purposes.
- It would mandate the highest standards of governance and accountability in the ILC, beyond those required in its Act or in the overarching public governance legislation. The reason for imposing higher standards on the ILC was to recognise it is the steward of moneys intended to compensate Indigenous Australians for dispossession and for the trading away of certain of our rights in the post-Mabo settlement.
- It seeks to enable the Land Account's capital base to increase over time, to cater for the growing Indigenous population.

A request from the Torres Strait Regional Authority that the ILC's remit be extended to sea in addition to land was supported in the ILC's submission to the Senate Community Affairs Legislation Committee.

The Minister for Indigenous Affairs refused to consider the draft Stronger Land Account Bill. The Australian Greens introduced it into the Senate and it was sent off to the Senate Community Affairs Legislation Committee where the government-dominated members recommended against it.

The Land Account remains fundamentally vulnerable. Parliament has the power to legislate to weaken its independence or to abolish it as we have seen with ATSIC. The minister has already weakened the level of Indigenous representation on the board by appointing a non-Indigenous person as deputy chairperson for the first time in the history of the ILC.

MOVING FRONTIER OF INDIGENOUS POLICY

The ILC's political travails over past two years are symptoms of wider problems—the way short-term aims affect matters of fundamental importance. The ILC board's attempt to get parliament to protect the Land Account through the Stronger Land Account Bill is just one part of a wider and continuing struggle.

In recent times within the Commonwealth Government, our first nations peoples have seen the weakening of legislation that goes to the core of our cultural heritage and identity, including the Native Title Act and the Aboriginal and Torres Strait Islander Heritage Protection Act. ATSIC was abolished and there have been serious attempts to amend the Racial Discrimination Act and the *Aboriginal Land Rights (Northern Territory) Act 1976.*

Paradoxically, by bringing the vast bulk of the Indigenous policy and program bureaucracy under one roof, close to the centre of power in Canberra, then Prime Minister Tony Abbott increased the risk of poor decision-making in respect of local communities and simultaneously reduced the opportunity for the voices of Aboriginal and Torres Strait Islander peoples and organisations to be heard.

With their half-a-billion-dollar cut to the budget for Indigenous programs under the auspice of streamlining the pre-existing multitude of government programs aimed at Closing the Gap, the Abbott Government in one stroke reinforced the centralised control that so many Indigenous leaders see as retrograde. It has undermined the responsibility of all other policy and service-delivery agencies, at both state and federal levels, to contribute to the government's Indigenous policy aspirations. The result has been policy and funding bottlenecks, and many governments and Australian Government agencies that should be held to account for poor results have been let off.

Indigenous Australians are as diverse in our own way as the wider Australian population. The challenges and opportunities we face are shaped by our individual and family histories. While our backgrounds, priorities, aspirations and concerns are united by common threads of cultural sophistication, attachment to country, dispossession and dispersal, we are nevertheless not one people, but many peoples. The policy challenges of a remote community such as Warburton or Wadeye are not those of Dubbo or Geraldton, or those of Redfern, Campbelltown or Fitzroy.

To be effective, Indigenous policy must be an astute combination of central co-ordination mixed with decentralised buy-in and ownership. It needs to ensure consistency and coherence in terms of policy principles and the application of nationally applied rights and responsibilities, while leaving space for local voices and local solutions.

To date, the present Australian Government, led previously by Tony Abbott and more recently by Malcolm Turnbull, has, more than most recent governments, failed to get this balance right. Indeed, my point is that it is arguable that no government in forty years has got it right.

There has been very little improvement since the Royal Commission into Aboriginal Deaths in Custody Report of 1991 and the Human Rights Commission's report from its National Inquiry into the Separation of Aboriginal and Torres Strait Islander Children from their Families. More recently, then Prime Minister Tony Abbott commented that the latest Closing the Gap report was 'in many respects profoundly disappointing'.

A HISTORY THAT CAN'T BE FORGOTTEN

On 31 October 2015, it was the fortieth anniversary of Australia's Racial Discrimination Act and, apart from a couple of media articles, there has been almost no coverage of its significance for Indigenous peoples. This lack of awareness or interest is of concern as Indigenous peoples pursue constitutional recognition. In addition to the fact that we are the original owners of this country, which should stand alone as the basis for recognition, the ongoing dispossession of our people requires it to be more than symbolic recognition.

It is important for people to know and have some appreciation that our first nations peoples were subjected to laws preventing us from voting, the freedom of movement, and equal wages as well as government policies including the forced removal from our lands and the forced removal of our children, and that these past and present policies have resulted in much of the dysfunction seen currently. Low expectations can be very powerful, and people often manage to live down to them.

CONSTITUTIONAL RECOGNITION

Indigenous peoples are relatively powerless in the face of the Australian state, a point that has been made strongly in recent debates about recognition of our first nations peoples in the Australian Constitution, and this does impact on the success or otherwise of policies, programs and service delivery.

The fear of judicial activism that currently haunts the debate is a spurious claim. To this end, the most significant threat for the wider Australian community and governments came following the Mabo (No 2) decision. Indigenous people clearly demonstrated their reasonableness and negotiated the 'Grand Bargain' and more recently negotiated settlement by the South West Aboriginal Land and Sea Councils of the West Australian Noongar claim.

A view that our first nations peoples 'should know their place', which started with the early Europeans' discovery of Australia and subsequent colonisation, is deeply embedded in the Australian psyche and is by far the most significant barrier to achieving meaningful recognition within the Constitution. The development of policies and enactment of legislation for our Indigenous peoples were based on the assumption we were an inferior race, and the adoption of the doctrine of *terra nullius* gave credence to this theory. The Hawke Government openly recognised the requirement for a broader attitudinal change in Australia if a treaty or compact was to be achieved. The reconciliation process since 1991 has been successful across a range of sectors but clearly not sufficiently enough to give government the comfort it requires to make any announcement on the questions to be put to the Australian public at referendum or the timing.

In recent times, this attitude goes to the issue of what the view of the broader and the mostly Anglo-Australian community believes is what it means to be Australian.

Indigenous dot paintings are acceptable as mainstream art and highly prized for decorating the walls of contemporary houses and offices but, by and large, the story and complexity of the culture that is the basis for the art is not recognised. The artwork created by Fiona Foley called *Annihilation of the Blacks* was strongly criticised by visitors to the National Museum of Australia. One person was moved to say they hated Fiona Foley's work and that it was unnecessary. This attitude reflects a lack of understanding of or acceptance that for Fiona Foley and many other Indigenous artists, the aesthetic expression and the demand for social justice and recognition are inextricably linked.

Cathy Freeman was subjected to vitriolic criticism from the Returned Services League and others in 1984 when she carried both the Australian and Aboriginal flags after she won gold at the Commonwealth Games in Canada. Following Freeman's win at the Sydney Olympics we could be forgiven if our first nations peoples were lulled into a false set of expectations that, perhaps, Anglo-Australians were now accepting that their sporting heroes are proud to be Indigenous and would want to display their indigeneity accordingly. However, as we have seen recently, there has been an ongoing hostile reaction to Adam Goodes proudly showcasing his Aboriginality by his 'invisible spear' dance.

AGAINST THE ODDS

Our first nations peoples have retained our identity as the original inhabitants of Australia, against the odds. Many who were disconnected from their traditional lands have been reunited because of the Racial Discrimination Act, the Aboriginal Land Rights (Northern Territory) Act and as a result of the impetus of Eddie Koiki Mabo and his fellow litigants and the subsequent negotiated settlement known as the 'Grand Bargain'. However, much damage has been done by the early laws and the ever-changing policies and programs in contemporary Australian politics, either because of change of government or because of the whim of a minister. Both of the major political parties place Indigenous affairs low in the priority order. The fact remains that Indigenous Australians are relatively powerless in the face of the Australian state, a point that has been made strongly in recent debates about recognition of Indigenous Australians in the Constitution.

Above all, I think that Indigenous Australians need protection from bad laws and the ideological fixations of governments, of whatever persuasion, or the personal agendas of ministers.

There is now a bipartisan commitment to Indigenous constitutional recognition. It is a logical next step in advancing Indigenous recognition and rights; it harks back to the unfinished business of the 1967 Referendum; it would be a landmark in the process of reconciliation; it would build on the act of recognition that was the Mabo judgement.

Most Australians seem to support recognition of Indigenous Australians, and would surely agree to the removal of the race power from the Constitution.

There are differing opinions in the Indigenous community, but also an overwhelming consensus that any constitutional change must go beyond symbolism. The Racial Discrimination Act, when not suspended as it was by the Howard Government, has proven to be an effective means of changing behaviour.

Therefore, the next step, given the experience of the past, the call for some mechanism to guarantee Indigenous rights, for some Indigenous power within the nation, is surely the correct one.

12

UNFINISHED BUSINESS

Nyunggai Warren Mundine

In the final years of the Second World War, the Allies established a unit known as the Monuments, Fine Arts and Archives (MFAA) section. Their mission was to save European culture from plunder and destruction. The MFAA worked to safeguard, find and ultimately return works of art, archives, documents, monuments, cultural treasures and other items of historic or cultural significance.

Their story was told in a book by Robert M Edsel and later dramatised in a movie called *The Monuments Men,* directed by George Clooney, who also played the lead character, Frank Stokes. In a pivotal scene of the movie, Stokes speaks to his men on the eve of their mission in Western Europe. And he says this:

This mission was never designed to succeed. If they're honest they would tell us that. They'd tell us that with this many people dying, who cares about art?

They're wrong. Because that's exactly what we're fighting for. For our culture and our way of life.

> You can wipe out a generation of people, you can burn their homes to the ground, and somehow they'll still come back. But if you destroy their achievements and their history, it's like they never existed. It's just ash floating.

The first peoples of the Australian continent have feared this for centuries. That our achievements and histories will be destroyed. That our culture and languages will be forgotten. That it will be like we never existed.

British colonisation was built on the myth of *terra nullius*—that Australia was the land of no one.

Under eighteenth-century international law, Britain could only claim outright ownership of territory if it was uninhabited. Obviously Australia was inhabited. Even the British could see that. But Britain assumed the inhabitants didn't claim ownership of the land. They saw nomads living in unstructured societies with no recognisable civic or legal systems, who moved seemingly randomly over vast areas but didn't claim any particular territory for themselves and didn't manage the land.

They were wrong. In 1788, there were hundreds of distinct societies across Australia, each with their own unique language, traditions, kinship systems and governance. They had trading routes and methods for navigating over long distances. They modified, and intervened in, the environment to improve food sources and availability. They had complex kinship systems defining both personal and civic rights and responsibilities. And each group knew what was their country and what was the country of another group. The *Oxford Dictionary* defines a nation as 'a large body of people united by common descent, history, culture, or language, inhabiting a particular state or territory'. This describes those societies exactly.

These were Australia's first nations and they are the oldest surviving nations in the world.

The High Court put an end to the notion of *terra nullius* in 1992 with the Mabo decision. This acknowledged that Australia's first peoples did in fact occupy, possess and enjoy particular areas of land and sea to the exclusion of others, and which were inherited by subsequent generations. This was the first time Australia's first nations were recognised by the Australian Commonwealth.

RECOGNITION IS MISSING THE POINT

The idea of recognising Indigenous Australians in the Constitution has been around for some time. Australians have, in fact, already voted on a proposal to recognise Indigenous people in the Constitution. During the Republic referendum in 1999, Australians voted on a new constitutional preamble that, among other things, honoured Indigenous Australians as

Australia's first peoples, their 'deep kinship with their lands' and 'ancient and continuing cultures'. This vote failed.

In 2007, Prime Minister John Howard announced that, if elected, the Coalition would again put a referendum to the Australian people within eighteen months to formally recognise Indigenous Australians in the Constitution as well as 'their history as the first inhabitants of our country, their unique heritage of language and culture, and their special, though not separate, place within a reconciled indivisible nation'. His goal was to have a new statement of reconciliation incorporated into the Constitution's preamble. Howard didn't get an opportunity to honour this commitment—within two months, the Coalition lost office.

On his second sitting day as Prime Minister, Kevin Rudd delivered the National Apology to the Stolen Generations. In that speech, he spoke about establishing a joint policy commission to work on the further task of constitutional recognition. Rudd, and later Prime Minister Julia Gillard, continued to push the idea forward during Labor's six years in office, including appointing experts to consider and recommend amendment proposals. Former Prime Minister Tony Abbott made constitutional recognition a genuine priority for his government when elected in 2013 and Prime Minister Malcolm Turnbull has continued the Coalition's Indigenous affairs policies.

Now, more than eight years after Howard's initial pledge, you'd be forgiven for thinking the constitutional recognition initiative has lost momentum. Arguably, it never had it.

In large part, this is because we've been talking about recognition for over a decade but we still don't know what we are talking about. We have had proposals to take race out of the Constitution; to put race back in; for constitutional human rights protections; for special Commonwealth powers over Indigenous people; to give constitutional status to Indigenous representative bodies; for a constitutional preamble. The list goes on. Many of these proposals go well beyond what is needed to recognise Australia's first nations. Some, to be blunt, are nothing more than solutions looking for a problem.

None of the proposals get to the nub of the issue. The nation of Australia was founded in 1901 when six British colonies agreed to unite as a federal Commonwealth under the Australian Constitution. The Constitution refers to Britain and the colonies, but doesn't mention the first nations of Australia that preceded them.

It's as if they never existed.

ABORIGINAL NATIONS

History demonstrates that for constitutional change to happen, the change must, at a minimum, capture the hearts and minds of the Australian people. Yet the push for recognition hasn't even captured the hearts and minds of Indigenous Australians. And it never will while it continues to be framed around the way others have looked at us, not around the way we look at ourselves; while it continues to be about recognising a race of people, rather than recognising first nations.

Indigenous Australians don't think of themselves as a 'race'. The only context in which the notion of race is front of mind for us is the context of racism.

I'm not part of an 'Aboriginal race' or a 'black race'. I'm an Australian. I'm also a member of the Bundjalung nation, the nation of my father and his ancestors going back tens of thousands of years and the country on which I was born. Through my mother, I'm descended from the Gumbaynggirr, Yuin and Irish nations, and I identify with those nations too.

The Bundjalung are not a race of people any more than Australians are a race of people. Nor are the Gumbaynggirr, Yuin or Irish. They are nations of people.

This distinction was illustrated to me during the Scottish vote for independence in 2014. Turning on the news one night, I saw a report on the Scottish referendum that opened with a group of black women singing for independence. They were proud Scots and they were black. Scotland is not a race. It's a nation. And it continues to be a nation despite voting to remain part of the United Kingdom, something Prime

Minister David Cameron acknowledged during the independence campaign.

British colonisation cut a swathe through the first nations of Australia. They had to adapt to new situations—outsiders on their country who were not under their kinship system; being moved off country to another nation or to mixed settlements with people from other nations; being prohibited from speaking their languages or practising ceremony. Some groups didn't survive intact. Those that did survived the way any nations do when under threat or upheaval—by preserving what they could of the old ways and by adapting to the new. But we did not forget or abandon our first nations—or to use our word, our mobs. One of the first questions Indigenous people ask each other when we meet for the first time is, 'Who's your mob?'

Indigenous Australians will always be united as kindred spirits in our shared history. Unity has made us stronger and more resilient, and as a united group we have achieved a great deal. But we will always be separate mobs first and foremost, with our distinct and unique country, heritage, languages and cultures.

The 2014 Social Justice and Native Title Report, released by the Aboriginal and Torres Strait Islander Social Justice Commissioner Mick Gooda, confirms this. In preparing the report, the commission spoke extensively with Indigenous people all over Australia. It found that Indigenous Australians overwhelmingly identify with their traditional nations over identifying as 'Aboriginal' or 'Indigenous'. The report stated:

> In the hearts and minds of Aboriginal and Torres Strait Islander peoples, our 'nationhood' has always survived and continues to be acknowledged between us.
>
> Some Nations remain strong, with traditional practice still being undertaken today.
>
> Other Nations have adapted traditional ways to meet modern standards.
>
> Sadly, some other Nations have been fractured or devastated.

Having observed and participated in the discussion about constitutional recognition for some years, I've come to the conclusion that any proposal for constitutional recognition that doesn't acknowledge the first nations of Australia won't capture the hearts and minds of Indigenous Australians, let alone the rest of Australia. And the more I think about it, the more I believe that the focus on the race powers of the Constitution is a red herring.

Indigenous Australians can be meaningfully recognised whether the race provisions remain in the Constitution or not. The Constitution's race provisions are not about Indigenous people. In fact, from 1901 to 1967 they expressly excluded us. From 1967, they became a means for the Commonwealth to take control of Indigenous affairs away from the states, a *de facto* Indigenous affairs power. This was a political consequence more than it was a legal consequence.

Few laws actually rely on the constitutional race power. Those that do arguably include laws about native title and Indigenous heritage protection. It would be a very cruel irony if constitutional recognition put those laws at risk. If the solution to that risk is to create constitutional powers to make laws for Indigenous people, then the solution is merely a race power by another name, and a discriminatory one at that. It would effectively take us back to 1966. Linking constitutional recognition to the race provisions reinforces the very mind-set Indigenous Australians have resisted for over two centuries.

The race powers are an archaic remnant of nineteenth-century thinking. But, since 1967, they have at least been race neutral. Everyone is potentially impacted by them. Perhaps race should be removed from the Constitution. Perhaps it's better to let sleeping dogs lie. Maybe it is a change worth fighting for. Maybe it's a fight for another time. But what we do about the race powers need not impact constitutional recognition one way or another. Because recognising Australia's first nations is not about race.

NATION TO NATION

The first nations of the Australian continent should have been acknowledged and recognised from the moment Britain set eyes on it. Eighteenth-century international law required that if territory was inhabited, Britain could either purchase land from the inhabitants or conquer it by force. Conquest did not extinguish the inhabitants' pre-existing rights to land, however. As a result, both avenues usually involved a treaty or agreement with the Indigenous people of that territory.

Britain signed numerous treaties across Polynesia, India, North America and Africa. But, having designated the Australian continent as uninhabited, Britain did not sign a treaty with its first nations. This remains unfinished business.

Calls for a treaty between Australia and Indigenous people have come and gone over the years. A very vocal push for a treaty was led by the National Aboriginal Conference (NAC) that, in 1979, called for the negotiation of a treaty between Aboriginal people and the Australian Government. The idea of a treaty reached a peak in 1988 when Prime Minister Bob Hawke promised his government would enter into a treaty with Indigenous people by 1990. This was never delivered. Hawke instead focused on the idea of 'reconciliation' between Indigenous and non-Indigenous Australians.

Today, the recognition and reconciliation initiatives underpin Indigenous policy and engagement at all levels. I believe that neither initiative can conclude its objectives if we don't revisit the idea of a treaty. A treaty marks the end of a conflict, draws a line in history and allows signatories to move on based on a clean slate. A treaty requires and brings about mutual recognition and reconciliation.

However, the notion of a treaty between Indigenous Australians as a single group and the Australian Government, as proposed by NAC and others since, will not work. When you get beyond the broad concept and start thinking about how to implement it, you realise there are no individuals who speak for Indigenous Australians as a single group.

Contrast NAC's 1979 proposal with the Yolngu bark petitions. In 1963, the Yolngu people issued a petition, presented on bark and signed by leaders of all the Yolngu clans. The petition objected to the government's grant of mining leases on Yolngu land without their consent and demanded Yolngu rights to land and sea be recognised. It was presented to federal parliament.

NAC's call for a treaty and the Yolngu's bark petitions were both effective in bringing attention to the campaign for Indigenous land rights and recognition. But they were different. NAC called for a treaty between Australia and Aboriginal people as one single group. The bark petitions were presented on behalf of the Yolngu people to the Australian Government, nation to nation. The petitions did not purport to represent the demands of non-Yolngu people. And they couldn't. Yolngu can speak only for Yolngu country; others must speak for their country.

Yolngu people to this day regard the bark petitions as speaking for them and their country. NAC's call for a treaty represented no one but NAC. Notwithstanding NAC being an elected body, NAC members did not and could not speak for any first nation of Australia. And even if NAC had been offered a treaty by the Australian Government and signed it, most Indigenous Australians would not regard that as speaking for them or their country.

To have any meaning, a treaty has to be between Australia and each first nation of Australia, nation to nation.

My proposal for recognition is very basic. The Australian Government should offer to enter into agreements with each first nation of Australia, recognising them as the traditional owners and custodians of their land and sea and as a first nation of Australia. As part of that agreement, their native title claims should be fast-tracked, accepted and concluded. The 'continuous connection to the land' condition of native title claims should also be dispensed with. The tribes and language groups of Aboriginal and Torres Strait Islander peoples have been extensively studied and documented. By and large, the country of each first nation is known, whether or not people have maintained a continuous connection to it. Many people lost their connection through no choice of their own.

Under this approach, individuals would be required to establish membership of that first nation to participate in its native title settlement and governance system.

At the same time, each first nation who signs on to the agreement should formally recognise the nation of Australia; they should be prepared to draw a line in history and move on as part of Australia as a whole based on a clean slate.

These agreements could be called treaties, or could be named using a word from the language of the first nation signatory.

As radical as this may sound, it's only a few steps beyond what is already happening. The Mabo decision recognised that native titleholders occupied particular areas of country to the exclusion of others. Native title groups already enter into Indigenous Land Use Agreements (ILUAs) that are binding agreements with governments, organisations and/or others regarding their native title and other matters. Once registered, ILUAs bind all native titleholders in the agreement area, even those who did not personally sign the ILUA. They are, in a sense, a form of treaty signed on behalf of a first nation of Australia.

SPEAK IN A LANGUAGE WE UNDERSTAND

The fact that Australia's Constitution does not acknowledge that societies existed on the Australian continent before the British colonies is a symptom of a much more fundamental oversight: the failure to acknowledge that Australia's first nations existed in the first place. That is the wrong that needs to be righted.

Nelson Mandela once said:

> If you speak in a language they understand, you speak to their head. If you speak in their own language you speak to their heart.

Talking about constitutional recognition of, or a treaty with, Indigenous Australians as a single group is like speaking to us in a language we understand. It speaks to our heads.

But talking about our traditional nations and recognising who can speak for country is like speaking to us in our own language, because that is how we think about ourselves. That is how you speak to our hearts.

The Australian continent is home to one of the youngest nations of the world—Australia—as well as to the oldest nations of the world—the first nations of Australia. All Australians can embrace and share in this rich and ancient history.

Constitutional recognition was an idea of the Australian Government. It was not a grassroots campaign originated by Indigenous Australians. What we have always wanted is the same thing the Yolngu petitioned for: that our rights over our own countries be recognised and respected. Of course the Constitution should acknowledge Australia's first Nations. What is even more important is that Australia acknowledges them.

13

CONSTITUTIONAL RECOGNITION IS NOT A FEEL-GOOD EXERCISE

Sean Gordon

Like many australians, I have been following recent media on Noel Pearson's proposals for Indigenous constitutional recognition. I agree that it is never too late for good ideas. The conversation must continue and nothing is settled.

Beyond that, my thoughts have been consumed by what a national Indigenous representative body would mean on the ground for my people on the Central Coast, as well as across Australia. I want recognition to make a real difference in achieving practical outcomes and securing economic development opportunities.

There is nothing I want more than economic development for our people. I want them to enjoy the same opportunities as everybody else. But there need to be structures in place for this to happen. In many cases we are doing everything we can to get ahead, but there are still many structural and social barriers to success.

Darkinjung Local Aboriginal Land Council (Darkinjung) is one of the lucky Indigenous entities. We are well resourced and we receive little government funding. We are pursuing economic development in our region. The resistance we face would surprise most people. In one recent development application, our proposal attracted 2200 objections—more than any other development in the history of the Central Coast.

Some objections had little substance. There were suggestions that the development would see dogs roaming around the place, or that it would bring drunks to the neighbourhood. Prejudice remains a practical obstacle to our people achieving success economically, socially and culturally. These attitudes influence the way in which local government decisions are made—because public views are important. It is clear that discrimination plays a significant role.

On top of that obstacle, we have to fund expensive court cases in the land and environment court for our rights to economic development. Each fight costs on average $200,000, which adds to the cost our organisation must bear. These funds could be better spent building homes or providing real benefits to our community. But what about other Indigenous communities across the country who are not as well resourced? How are they supposed to negotiate the expensive court system in order to prosecute their rights to a sustainable future and a viable community?

REFORM, NOT RECOGNITION

Symbolic recognition of Indigenous people in the Constitution will not be enough to drive reform, deliver development and build sustainable communities. If all recognition is going to do is make Australians feel good, then this debate is heading in the wrong direction and not going far enough.

On that basis, I am attracted to the proposal for an Indigenous body enshrined in the Constitution. I think it could help enable Indigenous empowerment and economic development. Such a body could drive law reform at a national level, removing the burden on individual Indigenous organisations to battle alone.

This kind of structure would enable Indigenous Australians to communicate and collaborate with government in order to find appropriate solutions—an alternative to constant litigation. Government would have an efficient way to hear Indigenous views about what needs to happen to encourage Indigenous economic success. It would also provide an avenue to encourage and recognise the Indigenous contribution to the economic future of the nation.

There is no better feeling than driving into a Darkinjung-owned residential development site and seeing our contribution to the local economy. For every

$1 million we spend, we create ten jobs. Ten per cent of our development is retained by Darkinjung for affordable housing for our members at no cost to taxpayers. I want to see more Indigenous communities achieving this kind of independence.

For this to happen, communities need to be able to tell government how to get rid of the barriers to their development. If there is no structural interface to allow our people to communicate with government, then there is no way they can succeed.

Designed properly, such a body could vastly improve the way the Indigenous space operates. Our small and under-resourced communities would not be so alone and isolated. They could have this national body, with local connections, taking their concerns and aspirations to Canberra. It could be a structure to empower Indigenous people to work together more effectively.

We all know that the nation faces the challenge of closing the gap between Indigenous Australians and non-Indigenous Australians. But the current debate goes on at such a high level. There is no structural connection between government and community. The question is: how do we empower communities to take ownership of solutions? The suggested Indigenous body could connect the high-level political debates to the local knowledge of our people on the ground.

Of course, economic development is not the only important thing. In New Zealand, there are structures for Maori representation in parliament and settlements under the Waitangi Tribunal, both of which increase potential for effective economic development. But they also have the Maori Language Commission to promote and revitalise Maori language and culture. We could have this type of institution in Australia too.

I would want to see the body not only drive economic development in the regions, but also to help with language, culture and place name recognition. Everything depends on how the structure is designed and what else makes up the proposed package of reforms. Indigenous Australians need to engage with this proposal. We need to start discussing the possibilities.

Future law reform should be properly informed and led by Indigenous people. Real, on-the-ground Indigenous involvement and communication with government will be crucial if we are going to close the gap and revitalise and maintain Indigenous heritage. On that basis, this deserves serious consideration.

The Empowered Communities initiative could complement such a structure. We could have an Indigenous representative voice at the constitutional level, and more efficient mechanisms for government engagement at the legislative and institutional levels.

BUILDING A SOLUTION TO OUR OWN PROBLEMS

The Empowered Communities initiative was engendered more than two years ago, when twenty-five Indigenous leaders gathered on the New South Wales Central Coast. As a group, we embodied the diversity of Aboriginal Australia. We came from and represented urban, regional and remote communities.

We were drawn together by our shared despair over the lack of progress made in improving the lot of our people. For us, this has always meant social, economic and cultural development: families and children living safely by a set of social values or norms; young people getting a good education and jobs and economic growth for our people. At the same time, we want our culture, heritage and languages to be retained and valued.

At the first meeting, as the macabre exercise of comparing miseries conjured an insurmountable mountain, an insight appeared. Our people, being the 3 per cent mouse of the population, are fragile and weak in our dealings with the might of government elephants. As leaders in communities and heads of organisations, we are largely powerless. For example, none of us have any clear sightlines into the funding that goes into our communities, funding that purports to be about solving the same issues for which we are seeking solutions. Yet we are not privy to how these resources are applied. The result is constant doubling up on some types of services, yawning gaps in other much-needed services, turf wars, money and resources frittered away for no gain, efforts that are making a difference easily abandoned, and efforts that are not effective remaining.

Animated by this simple insight, we set out to devise a plan. We did not want to simply ask government to fix it for us—that well-worn approach has not been working for decades. We took it on ourselves to find a better way. So, the Empowered Communities initiative was born.

Our work since then has been extensive. We have built and designed this new interface from the ground up. In the eight Empowered Communities regions, the landscape was carefully mapped to build a realistic picture of the dynamics, people, organisations and relationships that could deliver a cohesive and truly representative community voice. On the other side, with the assistance of current and former senior bureaucrats, the government landscape was mapped.

With these two sides of the coin understood, we designed an interface to take in the complexities and unique structures of different regions and convert these inputs into a balanced, cohesive and orderly process for governments to engage with. This, we strongly believe, can be the engine room for real change and better outcomes for Aboriginal people, no matter what their circumstance. We think it could save money and time in our efforts for the betterment of our people.

After eighteen months of intensive design work, we presented our Empowered Communities: Empowered Peoples Design Report to the federal government in March 2015. The report represents a deeply serious, studious and concerted effort by an unprecedented coalition of Indigenous leaders. It represents the pinnacle of their individual and collective thinking. The report is the apex of our thinking, the culmination of countless sleepless nights stretching back decades; it's the premier reply from us as leaders to the enduring question that besets our nation—why can't we close the gap?

STRUCTURAL CHANGE AND SELF-DETERMINATION

It is self-evident that the circumstance of the birth of Empowered Communities is superior to the haphazard and often glib ways that Indigenous policy has been formulated to date—with government making all the calls and little input from the Indigenous people on the ground and in the regions, who the government policies are supposed to benefit.

When we look at the big picture, it starts to feel exciting. We could have constitutional reform to enable an Indigenous voice in parliamentary and government processes at the national, Commonwealth level. We could have the appropriate legislative and institutional reforms to enable a more efficient, more effective working relationship between Indigenous peoples and the government at the bureaucratic, on-the-ground, service-delivery level.

Together it would mean a restructured national approach to Indigenous affairs, based on the working principles of Indigenous self-determination: the principle that Indigenous people should be making the decisions about the laws and policies and services designed to benefit them. Our people should be genuinely and specifically engaged in the solutions for our own development and prosperity, through structures that actively include and support our effective participation and leadership in the decisions that most affect our lives and communities.

This is of course a matter of justice for our people. But it is also a matter of practicality. If Australian governments are genuinely serious about the need to close the gap, the practical importance of Indigenous involvement and empowerment in Indigenous policy-making, lawmaking and service delivery cannot be denied. Either we as a nation are serious about the need to close the gap, and improve the circumstances of Indigenous people, or we are not.

The gap will not be closed, and Indigenous empowerment will not be achieved, through more of the same policies devised wholly by government and delivered to Indigenous people. A structural solution is required: one that gives Indigenous people a say, and increased authority and responsibility, over the decisions that affect us.

I wait with anticipation to see how the political leadership will respond to these two sensible requests from Indigenous people: two requests for structural change to ensure our people can take more authority and responsibility in our own affairs. Two requests for increased Indigenous self-determination. I am hoping with all my heart that Australia will move in the right direction.

14

IS THE CONSTITUTION A BETTER TOOL THAN SIMPLE LEGISLATION TO ADVANCE THE CAUSE OF AB ORIGINAL PEOPLES?

Michael Mansell

There seems to be an inexplicable fixation, an almost naive focus, on the Constitution as the mechanism for solving Aboriginal issues. The much-lauded 1967 Referendum transferred jurisdiction *over* Aboriginal people from state governments to the federal government. Aboriginal people are treated as subject matter for governments. Minor constitutional change does not challenge the right of parliaments to govern, or Aboriginal people the right to be governed.

More recent proposals have focused on 'recognition'.

The states of Queensland, New South Wales, Victoria, South Australia and now Western Australia have all given 'recognition' to Aboriginal people in their constitutions. Aboriginal people did not gain a single benefit from any of this. In 2013, the federal parliament passed the *Aboriginal and Torres Strait Islander Peoples Recognition Act 2013,* but apparently that was not recognition enough. The insatiable thirst for more recognition persists, perhaps revealing a deep insecurity among Aboriginal proponents and cheap conscience cleansing among its white supporters.

In context, 'recognise' has a strange connotation. We have never really needed to be recognised to establish the historical fact that we were always here. Nor were we 'discovered' by anyone because we were never lost. The inference is that unless Aboriginal people are somehow proclaimed by white people we are incomplete. It seems we ourselves cannot assert our legitimacy as a people unless white people recognise us. This has a tinge of inferiority about it.

In 2012, the report of the Expert Panel on Constitutional Recognition of Aboriginal and Torres Strait Islander Peoples stated recognition would improve the self-esteem of Aboriginal and Torres Strait Islander peoples and provide a better framework for the governance of the nation. It would bring Australians together, the panel believed, 'in a spirit of equality, recognition and respect and contribute to a truly reconciled nation'. This is abject nonsense.

How could four proposals—to make English the official language, put some nice words in the preamble, entrench anti-discrimination and repeal an obsolete section—reconcile a nation? Henry Reynolds lamented:

> We have never been one nation, popular rhetoric notwithstanding. We may never become one, at least not in the foreseeable future. We share a country, a continent and a state, but not a nation. [1]

Recognition supporters might misunderstand the purpose of the Constitution. The Australian Constitution converted former British colonies into States. Those States share powers with a federal parliament. The Constitution sets the limits of the powers of the parliaments and provides for a court to decide disputes that arise between them. Under Federation, parliaments often deal with the same subject matter affecting people, finances and land use and planning, so the Constitution provides demarcation lines. Significantly, the institutions established by the Constitution and the values they are based on all derive from England. Inserting some form of Indigenous recognition into this political arrangement cannot alter the arrangements, nor apparently is it meant to. For governments, it would be business as usual.

What is the goal here? Is this part of the assimilation program? The implication does not fit in with ATSIC chairman Geoff Clark advocating a treaty, or Pat Dodson wanting a political settlement. Nor does it sit well with Aboriginal leaders calling for an equitable sharing of power and land, and for Aboriginal self-determination. I have suggested thirteen designated seats in the Senate, not as an ultimate prize but as a means of gaining access to power. What will drive these changes and what legal mechanism can best deliver outcomes? All of these things can be legislated—quicker, more cheaply and with more certainty than through a referendum. Referenda are costly, time consuming and the outcome worse than uncertain, predictably unlikely to succeed. As Gary Foley said:

> Who gives a damn about whether we're mentioned in the Australian Constitution? What real difference will it make? It's a grand token gesture and will mean nothing in the long run, so it's a waste of time for people to be even talking about it. [2]

Legislation is the normal legal tool for changing rights and responsibilities in Western society. Constitutional amendments driven by Aboriginal people are anti-sovereignty: they endorse our status as mere citizens instead of as a distinct sovereign people. Merely asking for some vague reference in the Constitution is intellectually shallow and politically short-sighted. Would the Palestinians be satisfied with being merely acknowledged by Israel?

Inserting Aboriginal sovereignty or the indigenous right to self-determination into the Constitution is more principled but still has its problems. Unless the rights were intended to interfere with the division of powers between federal and state parliaments, the constitutional scheme of parliamentary supremacy would continue as normal. At best, mentioning Aboriginal sovereignty somewhere in the Constitution would simply acknowledge some form of previously held status. Unless it was intended to somehow alter the political arrangements, it would have no place and have no effect in the Constitution. As self-determination is more readily defined, and if it were inserted into Part V of the Constitution dealing with federal parliament powers and again in Chapter V dealing with State powers, it might burden the exercise of parliaments dealing with specific Aboriginal subject matter. It is risky. If the intention is to restrict powers of parliaments, then why not just legislate it?

I have written up a proposal for an Aboriginal State to be legislated by the Commonwealth under its section 121 constitutional power. The proposal is not really for an exclusive Aboriginal State because whoever resides within its proposed territory of 2.3 million square kilometres would have the same rights to participate in governing the territory as Aboriginal people. My State model also allows for Aboriginal people who do not reside on the territory of the new State to participate in it, including standing for its Assembly. These rights could be entrenched in the constitution of the new State.

If customary law were to be secured in the Aboriginal State, its Constitution would need to cement it as a source of law. Customary law is not recognised anywhere in Australia. White law prevails, regardless of the circumstances. The Northern Territory intervention laws went so far as to prohibit courts from taking customary law into account. The federal parliament has the sole power to establish new States and, after it legislates to do so, parliament thereafter lacks further power to un-legislate the State or interfere with the State Constitution. Importantly, the new State Constitution must have been in existence *at the time* parliament legislates the new State into existence. This brief background raises the issue of which Constitution needs most attention—a new Aboriginal State Constitution or the existing Australian Constitution? It might be time to prioritise.

No work is being done on the new State Constitution while attention is on recognition. Constitutional change proposals also release governments from dealing with land rights, heritage protection, seats in parliament, self-determination and statehood. In the meantime, at the drop of a hat, Aboriginal leaders will fly from one end of the country to the other to speak to politicians about the Australian Constitution.

The cost of a proposed referendum dealing with local government in 2013 was $55 million. The Australian Electoral Commission estimated it would cost in excess of $120 million to hold the vote on that issue separately. Any referendum on recognition in 2017 will cost a lot more. When Aboriginal communities and services have already been slashed by hundreds of millions of dollars, it puts a costly referendum, with uncertain outcomes, into sobering perspective.

Constitutionally entrenched anti-discrimination

Pat Dodson and the Expert Panel propose to ban racial discrimination in the Constitution itself by restricting federal parliament's use of the race power. The intention is to prevent parliament from having a power to pass racially discriminatory laws. The federal parliament is fast growing a reputation as the main discriminator against Aboriginal people, asylum seekers and Muslims.

The Expert Panel proposed an amendment to the Constitution to provide for a new section, possibly numbered 'section 116A', along the following lines:

1 The Commonwealth, a State or a Territory shall not discriminate on the grounds of race, colour or ethnic or national origin.

2 Subsection (1) does not preclude the making of laws or measures for the purpose of overcoming disadvantage, ameliorating the effects of past discrimination, or protecting the cultures, languages or heritage of any group.

It is not apparent why the proposal includes States and Territories. The *Racial Discrimination Act 1975* (Cth) is federal legislation. By virtue of section 109 of the Constitution (where there is inconsistency, Commonwealth law prevails over State laws), the Racial Discrimination Act already operates as a constitutional prohibition on States wanting to override the Racial Discrimination Act. The Commonwealth can also disallow Territory laws at any time.

The focus then is on the Commonwealth itself. The Racial Discrimination Act cannot prevent any federal parliament from passing a racist law where parliament has a power to do so. The Racial Discrimination Act cannot stop federal parliament suspending the operation of the Act at any time. It is clearly hoped that a constitutional ban might restrict the scope of the Commonwealth to pass racist legislation. It might, maybe...

The real problem with anti-discrimination measures is in allowing governments to carry on with day-to day business that sometimes has the unintended and incidental effect of discriminating against Aboriginal people. Where legislation has a legitimate purpose and impacts unfairly on a particular race but the discriminatory impact is incidental to its main purpose, the law will still be valid. There may be a legitimate reason for making a law—building a railway in South Australia where an Aboriginal burial ground is discovered—and harm to Aboriginal people is not its purpose, but an accidental by-product.

The approach of Australian courts is that the right to be free from racial discrimination must be balanced against other competing rights and values. Parliaments may therefore validly legislate even where the impact on Aboriginal people is discriminatory. Not all acts of racial discrimination are unlawful. People are hauled before courts for stealing while Aboriginal dispossession has no remedy. The white Australian passport is valid under Australian immigration laws but the Aboriginal passport is not.

Laws can even validly discriminate where they directly target Aboriginal people. In 2008, the Queensland Parliament passed a law restricting consumption of alcohol on Palm Island, where nearly all the residents are Aboriginal people. Police armed with guns and tasers then proceeded to search residents' and visitors' bags, shopping and prams for grog. It is a scene not repeated in white communities. The government claimed the measure was 'for the purpose of overcoming disadvantage'. In other words, the law had a legitimate purpose and the obvious racial discrimination was incidental. The courts agreed, accepting that discrimination against Aboriginal people is permissible under the 'exceptions' or positive measures section of the Racial Discrimination Act.

An Aboriginal campsite in Western Australia was declared a reserve in 1994 for the 'use and benefit of Aboriginal Inhabitants'. Accusations of widespread child sexual abuse against one of its members led the government in 2003 to shut the reserve down in order to protect children. The single perpetrator was convicted and jailed. The whole Aboriginal community was disbanded and all Aboriginal families evicted. The government said this was a positive measure and the court agreed. Was it?

The criminal law convicted the single offender, so why were other black families punished? Why did the anti-discrimination laws not protect all Aboriginal people from being evicted from the camp, especially where the West Australian Government took advantage of social hysteria, inflamed by media? When a white girl was murdered and raped in the nearby Canning Vale Shopping Centre in Perth, the shopping centre was not closed down. When rape and domestic violence take place in a street or suburb of white residents, the community is not dismantled.

If laws clearly discriminating against Aboriginal people are valid now under existing provisions that are to be copied into the Constitution, how could the result be any different? The proposal from the Expert Panel includes the 'escape' clause of positive measure.

President of the Queensland Court of Appeal Justice Margaret McMurdo considered a law that discriminates against Aboriginal people, intentionally or not, should be invalid. It can only be valid where it has the character of a special benefit, such as restricting alcohol consumption so that women and children subjected to violence are free to enjoy their human rights too. How, though, is a measure to be characterised as good or bad?

Is it irrelevant that the group deciding the character of the measure is a white parliament, and the body interpreting the measure is a white court? Where the State intends to intervene against Aboriginal people to save other Aboriginal people, should outsiders decide who is to be saved? One argument is to allow the group itself to decide. Only then can government act. But how is community consent to be ascertained? When considering 'positive' measures to restrict alcohol other than light beer, lawyers for the Queensland Government asked if they should get the consent of drunks to a liquor restriction law. What if the community is divided, as it apparently was in the Palm Island alcohol case?

In the Palm Island alcohol case, the court accepted that consultation with the Palm Island Justice Group, the Shire Council, police and the department responsible for Indigenous policy had taken place, although there was no final agreement on the alcohol restrictions. The compromise was to limit personal possession to thirty cans of mid-strength beer. Obviously not every resident was happy, otherwise the matter would not have made it to court. In the event, the court preferred the government claim that genuine attempts had been made at consultation despite the contrary views put directly by some Aboriginal residents.

It is not easy where the human right to be free from racial discrimination must be balanced against competing rights of women and children to grow up in a safe environment. Perhaps it is time to accept the Racial Discrimination Act is no longer worth pursuing as a remedial tool.

Academic and Aboriginal rights activist Gracelyn Smallwood believes the focus on the symptom rather than on the underlying causes explain why people, governments and courts struggle with the Racial Discrimination Act, saying:

> I guarantee you if the government fixed poverty in Aboriginal communities, 80 per cent of the violence and other problems would disappear. [3]

If Aboriginal people cannot be an effective part of government, the next best thing is to hold government accountable for the way it treats the people it governs. Federal legislation could impose an obligation on governments to relieve poverty in Aboriginal communities, judged by a standard laid down in the legislation itself. Independent bodies, preferably national and regional Indigenous ones, could monitor and report on progress. Alternatively it could be monitored by the Productivity Commission. It would be essential for the legislation to provide for Aboriginal people to sue government for failure to make reasonable efforts to make advances and comply with the legislation.

The proposed constitutional restriction on the use of the race power does not confer enforceable rights on Aboriginal people, nor does it impose any obligations on governments to take particular measures Aboriginal people want. It only operates as a shield, not a sword. The best it can do is protect against further discrimination, and even that is doubtful. Would it prevent cashless welfare cards being imposed, or coercing children away from their communities to attend city schools? As ideal as a constitutional ban on racism is, more thought is needed on whether leaving parliaments to decide what is best for Aboriginal people is indeed what is best for Aboriginal people.

A CONSTITUTIONALLY ENTRENCHED BODY

Another constitutional change proposed by Noel Pearson is for a constitutionally entrenched Aboriginal body to comment on federal legislation. Noel Pearson reasoned that if Aboriginal people could not prevent the parliament from making a bad law, they should at least have a say on what parliament is about to do. This seeks an indirect influence. Relying purely on moral persuasion and rational argument, matters politicians usually ignore, the proposal is not a strong one. The lack of imagination among Australia's political leaders forces Aboriginal leaders to seek minimalist change just to get a hearing. This is probably one such case.

Aboriginal people should be able to make decisions that bind governments, not the other way round. Legislate it. A 'right to comment' can be ignored and dismissed. Anyway, the proposed new body duplicates the existing function of the full-time Social Justice Commissioner whose role was described by the

Australian Human Rights Commission as 'reviewing the impact of laws and policies on Indigenous peoples'.

The Social Justice Commissioner was established in 1992 and seems fairly ineffective. It is hard to see the value in doing more of the same. Furthermore, a mere 'right to comment' endorses the right of politicians to decide while Aboriginal people can only comment.

Aboriginal people need affirmative action. If the Constitution must be altered, it should create an immediate benefit that imposes obligations on governments to act in a certain way. Aboriginal people should have a right to sue for breach. Instead of transferring decision-making to Aboriginal people, all constitutional proposals so far suggested leave it to parliaments to decide what is in the interests of Aboriginal people, while not advancing any form of Aboriginal decision-making.

If the issue is discrimination, dispossession or a treaty, legislation can specifically deal with it. If the problem persists, amending the legislation is a lot easier than constitutional change. It is true that legislation can later be repealed. But the *Aboriginal Land Rights (Northern Territory) Act 1976* is forty years old. New South Wales land rights laws were passed in 1983 and for Lake Condah and Framlingham in Victoria in 1987. Those laws still exist.

Legislation is more specific, can be worded to convey the intention behind it and can be changed later if need be. A successful referendum is harder to get than legislation. And the effect of a successful constitutional change is fraught with legal difficulties of subsequent interpretation. Who would have predicted the successful 1967 Referendum would be used against Aboriginal people?

15

KEEPING THE FIGHT ALIVE

Teela Reid

Recognition of aboriginal and Torres Strait Islander peoples as the 'First Peoples of Australia' cannot, and should not, be limited to constitutional reform. Since the announcement of the campaign for constitutional recognition in 2010, there has been strong support for change, although a wave of resistance has emerged primarily for two reasons. First, the absence of a model for a referendum and, second, the lack of investment in alternative views on how first peoples ought to *be* recognised. I therefore propose three practical and progressive ideas of my vision for our peoples and all Australians. They are: a treaty (or treaties), a bill of rights and a republic Australia.

To begin, when I met Riverbank Frank, a Wiradjuri and Gamiliroi Elder, in my final year of studying law, I was empowered to be courageous. He told me something I'd never heard an Elder say before: 'Culture ain't gonna save us.' Initially perplexed, I soon realised how wise his words were when thinking deeper about the manner and form of recognition for first peoples and the fundamental human rights that cross cultures. Below is an extract from Riverbank's poem, 'The Message':

We can all share
Australia's glory
I'm Wiradjuri/Gamiliroi
What's your story?

The best thing about
Australia to me
Has to be Diversity,
We're all different
But we are all one
This is our place
In the sun.

I hope some day
That we all will see
That we're the answer
You and me

Ain't black or white
It's humanity
Let's work together
To end race insanity. [1]

RACE RELATIONS

The relationship between the state and first peoples has been a tumultuous one, premised on racial discrimination. From the outset, Indigenous peoples were excluded from the Constitution and deemed a dying race. Then came the protection policies and the assimilation era, both of which were based on the narrative that Australia was peacefully settled. This is untrue. Australia is the only liberal democracy not to have entered a negotiation or settlement process. The issue has never been addressed by the parliament. Instead, the assumption that Australia was settled with the arrival of the British colony is deeply ingrained in the Australian psyche.

Whether Australia was invaded, conquered or settled is at the core of the current tension in the constitutional reform debate. Symbolic recognition of first peoples in a preamble of the Constitution—a Constitution that effectively came into force through an Act of the British Parliament—carries the risk of being viewed by the polity as a tacit acceptance of the settlement presumption. Symbolic recognition in the Constitution would not override a treaty, but it could delay a treaty process.

In 1788, when our ancestors were forced to fight for their traditional lands and territories, there was no constitution. When the Constitution came into force, there was *no recognition* of our ancestors as the first peoples, because we were expected to either die or get over it. The 1967 Referendum amended the Constitution to hand to the federal government the power to legislate with respect to Aboriginal and Torres Strait Islander peoples, a power that previously resided with the colonies. The amendment did not provide

Aboriginal and Torres Strait Islander peoples an opportunity to participate in public institutions' decision-making processes, despite the race power in the Constitution being used only in relation to Indigenous peoples. It is easy to see why first peoples have a complex and problematic relationship with the Constitution.

The sense of euphoria that flowed from 1967 soon diminished when laws and policies were interpreted so as to operate to the detriment of the Aboriginal and Torres Strait Islander peoples, as well as to their benefit. This was held in *Koowarta v Bjelke-Petersen* (1982) 153 CLR 168, and reaffirmed in *Kartinyeri v Commonwealth of Australia* (1998) 195 CLR 337, also known as the Hindmarsh Bridge Case. To rectify the power that enables the government to pass negative laws to the detriment of Aboriginal and Torres Strait Islander peoples, structural reform, not symbolism, is necessary. The Expert Panel on Constitutional Recognition of Aboriginal and Torres Strait Islander Peoples recommended a non-discrimination clause that ought to be considered in a model if a constitutional recognition referendum were to go ahead. This would not be a radical change given non-discrimination protections already exist within the *Racial Discrimination Act 1975* (Cth).

Reform, though, should not be limited to constitutional recognition. To limit recognition in this way would deny Aboriginal and Torres Strait Islander peoples the legitimacy as the first peoples to engage equally in a process of negotiation—something that was denied upon the invasion of our lands and territories from the outset. In moving forward, first peoples should have an opportunity to propose solutions outside constitutional reform, and the polity should not be misled by a one-sided government agenda. The overwhelming goodwill of non-Indigenous supporters should also be given the opportunity to engage with alternative views.

TREATY

There is no reason why recognising Aboriginal and Torres Strait Islander peoples as the first peoples in a treaty or treaties, as opposed to or as well as the Constitution, is not achievable. A treaty provides a mechanism outside the Constitution to reformulate the relationship between the state and first peoples, a reformulation that may ameliorate tensions around the settlement presumption. Given there is bipartisan support for symbolic recognition, a treaty could replace a referendum process, providing there is political leadership ensured by the prime minister. A treaty is a genuine step towards social justice and a pivotal moment in redefining Australia's national identity.

A treaty is a written agreement between the state and Indigenous peoples to recognise the place of first peoples in Australia's constitutional system, [2] to be equal before the law and to freely exercise their democratic rights. The terms of a treaty should be negotiated between first peoples and the state, and should implement the right to self-determination in accordance with Australia's international obligations under the *United Nations Declaration on the Rights of Indigenous Peoples* (UNDRIP).

A single treaty that implements the terms of the UNDRIP and is signed by the various first nations is a reasonably efficient process. Given the UNDRIP's universal application, international law experts like Professor Megan Davis could advise on the terms of a treaty relevant to Australia's historical context. Various members of first nations groups are familiar with international processes and the UNDRIP, which means this wouldn't be an abstract operation.

Fundamentally, a treaty would acknowledge cultural, social and economic rights and operationalise Indigenous peoples' rights to self-determination; to participate in decisions that affect their interests; to exercise choices over one's life; and to participate equally in the democratic process. A treaty would set out to achieve objectives identified by the Recognition, Rights and Reform report in 1995, including:

> a fairer, more prosperous and just society for all Australians. It is aimed at expanding choices and opportunities so all can participate as citizens in Australia's economic, social and political life and be better able to determine the direction of their own lives.

> [The] focus is on institutional, structural, collaborative, cooperative reform. It is about a fundamental shift from welfare to basic rights, from dependence to autonomy, from government assistance to power. Central to the social justice agenda is self-determination. [3]

A treaty is relevant and achievable and should not be dismissed as too ambitious. Such an agreement would lead to better decisionmaking processes by parliamentarians and would provide an effective national framework for how the state engages Indigenous peoples. In this way, a treaty is not a challenge to state sovereignty; it simply declares Indigenous sovereignty was never ceded through recognising Aboriginal and Torres Strait Islander peoples as the first peoples.

BILL OF RIGHTS

Following a treaty agreement that addresses the settlement presumption, entrenching a bill of rights would rectify racial discrimination in the Constitution. It would ensure all rights apply equally to all Australians and would subsequently remove racial discrimination from the Constitution. Among other fundamental freedoms, a bill of rights should entrench a clause giving effect to the self-determination of the first peoples—a clause that would not only have a legal effect, but additionally, and importantly, an educative effect, through the referendum process. [4]

The argument that rights are already equally applied and protected in the Australian democracy is flawed. The power to legislate against Aboriginal and Torres Strait Islander peoples is a clear example that basic democratic rights are not universal. Without legal protection in a bill of rights, federal, state and territory parliaments can abrogate many of our basic freedoms. A legislative instrument or charter of rights is also an ineffective measure to protect the rights of all citizens—this was demonstrated by the suspension of the *Racial Discrimination Act 1975* (Cth) to amend the *Native Title Act 1993,* to enact the *Hindmarsh Island Bridge Act 1997* (Cth), and to implement the Northern Territory Intervention in 2007. Coincidently, this has only ever occurred in the context of asserting control and breaching the fundamental rights and freedoms of the first peoples.

The discomfort with rights promotion in Australia is further proliferated by lack of leadership to understand rights, exaggerated by reactionary policies; for example, the Abbott Government's reactionary policies to 'Stop the Boats', to strip dual citizens of their Australian citizenship and to criminalise whistleblowers. These reactionary policies threaten our rights to life, privacy and free speech. According to Julian Burnside AO QC, Australians 'don't actually understand what rights are', [5] which could explain the lack of rights discourse and the insidious reluctance of many Australians to engage with this as a potential solution. Burnside warns that anyone who is willing to sacrifice rights for national security will 'end up with neither security nor liberty'. [6]

Without understanding the significance of rights and their universality, Australia cannot truly claim that it is 'better at protecting civil liberties'. [7] The argument against entrenching a bill of rights because it would transfer rights from the democratic process to the judiciary is also contestable: the judiciary's role is to interpret the law in its broader context. Importantly, where competing interests arise, for example state versus first peoples, the High Court applies a proportionality test to ensure state objectives are *balanced* against other interests. In this manner, the judiciary is more adaptable to interpret the exercise of rights in an Indigenous versus non-Indigenous context. While rights are universal, international laws such as the UNDRIP may 'give effect' [8] to rights consistent with Australia's international obligations.

AN AUSTRALIAN REPUBLIC

The next step, following treaty and a bill of rights, in creating a more unified nation would be Australia becoming a republic. A new republic referendum needs to avoid the pitfalls of the 1999 attempt, which failed primarily because there was no consensus on the model, under which the head of state would be appointed by parliament, not the voters. At that time, voters were also asked to change the preamble to recognise Aboriginal and Torres Strait Islanders as the first peoples. [9] The appeal of a republic is that it represents a move away from colonial heritage that burgeons the outdated 'Team Australia' vibe.

For Australia to become a republic, it would require a shift from conservatism to more progressive political plans. Australian legal ties to England have been severed as a result of the *Australia Act 1986* (Cth).It makes no sense to cling to the conflicting ideals imposed under the current Constitution that makes a non-Australian—the British Queen—our head of state. [10] Our head of state, or indeed a president of Australia, could well be an Aboriginal or Torres Strait Islander person. A republic referendum model should:

- remove the British Queen as head of state;
- insert in a preamble recognition that Aboriginal and Torres Strait Islander peoples are the 'First Peoples of the Republic of Australia';
- insert a treaty of first peoples; and
- dedicate compulsory seats for Aboriginal and Torres Strait Islander peoples in the House of Representatives and the Senate, or allocate one seat for an Aboriginal and Torres Strait Islander representative from each state and territory, or allocate one seat for a representative from each mob or group of peoples including Nyoongar, Wongi, Yamatji, Koori, Koorie, Goori, Murri, Pallawah, Torres Strait Islander, Yolngu, Anangu,

Nungas, Ngunnawai, Yapa, Tiwi, Murrdi, Bininji, Anindilyakwa, and so on.

A consequence of this process would be for each jurisdiction to provide for compulsory Aboriginal and Torres Strait Islander representative seats at a state and territory level.

The benefit of a republic is both structural and symbolic. National conversations about a new flag and national anthem are powerful changes signifying Australia is capable of evolving in a unified way that truly represents the diversity of the nation we have become.

Until this day, we must be willing to fight for nothing less than our ancestors fought for.

16

THERE'S NO SUCH THING AS MINIMAL RECOGNITION—THERE IS ONLY RECOGNITION

Noel Pearson

We have no righteous leader languishing in a Birmingham jail. But the 3 per cent of citizens of this country who are Indigenous represent 27 per cent of the total incarcerated in Australian prisons. This is worse than the incarceration of Martin Luther King Jr's people fifty years after Civil Rights: though African–Americans are about 12 per cent of the American population, they make up 40 per cent of the prison population. There is no Bull Connor enforcing our exclusion, but we have well-meaning priests, both secular and religious, cautioning against impatience and over-reach in our pursuit of constitutional recognition.

Unless the Australian nation holds some special hypothesis about the innate criminality of its Indigenous peoples, then what Ta-Nehisi Coates, author of *Between the World and Me,* calls the 'incarceral state' [1] cannot speak more clearly to the truth that there is a basic democratic problem in our country. Unless this nation continues to harbour that old pseudo-scientific belief in the inferiority of its Indigenous peoples—for some a matter of romantic tragedy and for others an unsentimentally brutal truth—then there is something wrong with the nation as a whole, rather than with the parlous minority.

The appalling incarceration numbers may be said to be the accumulation of long rap sheets of individual wrongdoing, but how can it be denied these individuals are not just random Australians with a pronounced propensity for ill-behaviour, but members, also, of a profoundly wronged people? Inasmuch as there are accumulated records of individual wrongdoing that necessarily yield a response in justice, there is also an accumulated record of historical wrongs—for which there has yet been no justice.

Those who came to take possession of Indigenous lands, and did so without consent, unilaterally decided the place that the dispossessed would take in the new nation they created. That place has not worked out well. It is a place that has kept the descendants of once-proud tribal nations behind bars in a society that, for most of its non-Indigenous citizens, is largely prosperous and free.

How can the structural dimension to Indigenous incarceration be any more apparent and yet subject to such obscurantism? There is something wrong in the Australian nation for us to even call it a 'situation' rather than the structural crime it really is. Martin Luther King Jr, from his jail cell in Birmingham, could well have written his letter on behalf of his antipodean brothers and sisters a half century later:

> We have waited for more than three hundred and forty years for our God-given and constitutional rights. The nations of Asia and Africa are moving with jetlike speed toward the goal of political independence, and we still creep at horse-and-buggy pace toward the gaining of a cup of coffee at a lunch counter. I guess it is easy for those who have never felt the stinging darts of segregation to say 'wait.' But when you have seen vicious mobs lynch your mothers and fathers at will and drown your sisters and brothers at whim; when you have seen hate-filled policemen curse, kick, brutalize, and even kill your black brothers and sisters with impunity; when you see the vast majority of your twenty million Negro brothers smothering in an airtight cage of poverty in the midst of an affluent society; when you suddenly find your tongue twisted and your speech stammering as you seek to explain to your six-year-old daughter why she cannot go to the public amusement park that has just been advertised on television, and see tears welling up in her little eyes when she is told that Funtown is closed to colored children, and see the

> depressing clouds of inferiority begin to form in her little mental sky, and see her begin to distort her little personality by unconsciously developing a bitterness toward white people; when you have to concoct an answer for a five-year-old son asking in agonizing pathos, 'Daddy, why do white people treat colored people so mean?'; when you take a cross-country drive and find it necessary to sleep night after night in the uncomfortable corners of your automobile because no motel will accept you; when you are humiliated day in and day out by nagging signs reading 'white' and 'colored'; when your first name becomes 'nigger' and your middle name becomes 'boy' (however old you are) and your last name becomes 'John,' and when your wife and mother are never given the respected title 'Mrs.'; when you are harried by day and haunted by night by the fact that you are a Negro, living constantly at tiptoe stance, never quite knowing what to expect next, and plagued with inner fears and outer resentments; when you are forever fighting a degenerating sense of 'nobodyness'—then you will understand why we find it difficult to wait. [2]

That seething impatience for justice is a feeling with which many Indigenous peoples are intimately familiar. It is the torment of powerlessness that drives advocacy for constitutional reform.

Indigenous Australians have now waited 228 years for our God-given and constitutional rights. We have watched comparable countries like New Zealand, Canada and the United States, move towards the goal of self-determination for their first nations peoples. The throne in Canada recently committed, 'because it is both the right thing to do and a certain path to economic growth' to 'renew, nation-to-nation, the relationship between Canada and indigenous peoples, one based on recognition of rights, respect, co-operation and partnership'. Is there a better articulation of what constitutional recognition of Indigenous peoples in Australia aspires to achieve?

Recognition means 'recognition of rights, respect, co-operation and partnership in the relationship between Indigenous first nations and the Australian state'. But while Canada seeks to renew and revitalise its first nations' constitutionally recognised treaty rights, Australia still moves at horse-and-buggy pace—and mostly around in circles. Those at the reins are so concerned about 'scaring the horses' that they forget about steering the carriage to any worthwhile destination. Tread softly, they tell us. Perhaps something better can be achieved in decades to come.

It may be easy for those who have never felt the stinging darts of racism and degradation in their own homeland to say 'wait'. But when your people continue to lose the land that was for millennia their birthright and you witness the steady decline of their once-rich cultures and languages; when they reside in an airtight cage of poverty in the middle of this affluent society; when so many are destined for jail and their children risk growing up with the same depressing clouds of inferiority forming in their mental skies that you yourself grew up with; when your people are plagued with national 'nobodyness', for they still lack a rightful place in this—our own country—perhaps then, one might understand why Indigenous peoples find it difficult to wait.

Proponents of same-sex marriage in Australia are impatient for recognition of same-sex marriage. For them civil union will not do; that is too tokenistic and doesn't go far enough. There is no persuasive argument that gay people should accept partial recognition now, in the hope of achieving full recognition at some later date—that would be bad politics and bad strategy. There can be no such thing as partial recognition of gay marriage.

Similarly, gay marriage proponents seek more than a symbolic statement of the equal worth and dignity of gay people and relationships. They do not seek some kind of well-meaning gesture of no practical consequence. They seek reform: tangible, substantive change in the rights of gay people under the law. There can be no such thing as minimalist or merely symbolic recognition of gay marriage.

Equally, there can be no minimalist or merely symbolic recognition of Indigenous peoples.

Indigenous people seek practical reform, not mere symbolism. It would be bad politics and bad strategy to accept a mediocre, tokenistic result in the fanciful hope of achieving fulsome recognition down the track, as some urge.

Indigenous people must decide what fulsome recognition means for us. In doing so, we should keep our principles and intentions high.

RE-IMAGINING SETTLEMENT

A good prism through which to explore the question is to imagine what the Australian first nations might have negotiated had attitudes of *terra nullius* not prevailed—had we been treated as sovereign peoples and the rightful owners of the land in the lead-up to Federation.

Had Indigenous peoples been afforded a place at the negotiating table during the decade of constitutional negotiations that preceded 1901, what might we have insisted upon? And what might we have strategically let go or exchanged in the face of the military might of the colonisers, who inevitably had the power and control? It would have been a King-like exercise: negotiating power and freedom from a position of powerlessness in the face of might.

Indigenous input into constitutional negotiations would not have been wasted on facile discussion of a minimalist preamble. Not while everyone else was arguing about rules, rights and representation, the terms upon which the new nation was to be governed. Not while the colonies insisted on equal representation in the senate and guarantees against inter-state discrimination. Standing in the face of the usurpers, the keepers of the English law that had, according to the judges in *Mabo,* washed like a tidal wave over their lands back in 1788 bringing with it Crown sovereignty and Indigenous devastation—could our proud tribal Elders have talked about anything other than the legal and political rights of their people under the new Constitution?

The first nations of Australia would have argued out the parameters and conditions for their inclusion in the union, too. Perhaps they would have carved out spheres of autonomy, guaranteed themselves equality, or negotiated a treaty setting out relevant matters. One thing would have been certain: our ancestors would not have negotiated ourselves three lines of decorative effect in a document that is fundamentally about the distribution of power and freedom. We would have negotiated ourselves some power. We would have negotiated ourselves some freedom to continue to exist in the new nation.

That, in my view, is the correct test for recognition of Indigenous peoples that is worth fighting for. That is the difference between mere symbolism and a practical reform of practical benefit. Reforms that involve an increase in power—by giving Indigenous peoples an increased voice, participation, authority, or representation in our affairs—or reforms that involve an increase in freedom—by guaranteeing us freedom from discrimination, for example. These are reforms that we should think deeply and carefully about. These are reforms worth pursuing. These are reforms worthy of constitutional amendment. A recognition proposition that involves no practical reform, no shift in power and no increase in freedom is a red herring and a false offer. It would amount to beads and trinkets.

The diplomatic process Indigenous peoples must now pursue should be one that takes into account the existing constitutional circumstances and our existing political position. It must be an approach that pragmatically acknowledges the political realities and the inherent difficulty of constitutional change—which requires multi-party political support and the support of all Australians.

But there can be no such thing as minimalist, half-hearted recognition. We are more empowered than we were in the 1800s. We cannot be excluded. Neither will we accept beads and trinkets. There are lawyers, politicians, teachers and scholars among us. Among us we have the skills to negotiate a just outcome. We must not sell ourselves short.

ASSIMILATION, FRAGMENTATION OR RECOGNITION?

One answer to Indigenous requests for recognition is for the rest of Australia to simply say 'No' and to insist on complete assimilation. The other extreme answer, for which some misguidedly argue, is to say 'Yes' but to insist on complete separatism and fragmentation—Indigenous peoples must detach from Australia completely and somehow form a separate nation. Neither extreme response is humane or sensible.

In reality, recognition is the middle way between complete assimilation and disappearance of Indigenous identity, and total separatism and fragmentation of the state. Many Western democracies are multinational, in that they are home to distinct nations or peoples who did not originally consent to the colonial power under which they are now governed. All those Western democracies now take measures for appropriate recognition and accommodation of those nations or peoples, so they can exist and prosper within the settler state in a way that is ethical, humane and peaceful—measures to ensure that those peoples can engage and participate in the nation in a way that is fairer and more inclusive than it has been in the past.

Australia must find our own middle way for recognition.

RIGHTS, REPRESENTATION, AGREEMENTS

Comparable liberal democracies reconcile the legal and political positions of Indigenous peoples within their settler states in different and unique ways that are appropriate and adapted to the country's particular historical, political and constitutional circumstances. Each nation finds its own ways to reconcile equality with difference: to accommodate the differentiated historical, legal and political positions of Indigenous peoples, and the rights arising therefrom, with liberal–democratic values and equal citizenship.

Broadly speaking, the reforms implemented by Western liberal–democratic nations to recognise, accommodate and protect the rights and interests of Indigenous peoples fall into three categories:

1 rights protection: bills of rights and constitutional guarantees;

2 representation: reserved seats and representative bodies; and

3 agreements: treaties and agreement-making.

RIGHTS

Declarations of rights in bills of rights and constitutional rights clauses are common forms of legal protection afforded to Indigenous minority groups within liberal–democratic nations. The Canadian Bill of Rights contains explicit protection of Indigenous treaty rights as well as an equality before the law protection. The US Bill of Rights also contains an equal protection clause and a clause prohibiting slavery. Most Western constitutions contain equality provisions, prohibiting racial and other forms of discrimination. New Zealand and the United Kingdom have unentrenched human rights acts. Australia lacks a legislated bill of rights, but we also lack any constitutional protection of equality before the law. Similarly, our Constitution lacks any clauses protecting distinct Indigenous rights and interests.

Rights protection through bills of rights and constitutional guarantees represents legal forms of constitutional protection. If the rights clause is constitutionalised in an entrenched constitution, it can mean that laws are struck down where they are found to breach the rights clause. Constitutional systems that include heavy reliance on a bill of rights or judicially interpreted constitutional guarantees create a framework for ongoing dialogue between the legislature and the courts, in order to protect the array of citizens' rights, including Indigenous rights.

REPRESENTATION

Representation is also often implemented as a form of Indigenous rights protection in comparable liberal democracies. New Zealand has had reserved Maori parliamentary seats since 1867, which are today proportional to the number of Maori in the population. Additionally, they have the Maori Council, a national representative body for Maori advocacy and community consultation on Maori affairs. The state of Maine in the United States also has reserved Indigenous parliamentary seats. In Norway, Sweden and Finland there are Sami parliaments, which act as indigenous advisory bodies empowered to engage with parliament.

Rather than transferring power to the judiciary as a form of legal protection of Indigenous rights, representative mechanisms, such as reserved seats and advisory bodies, can be understood as political and procedural mechanisms for Indigenous rights protection within constitutional arrangements. Rather than creating a dialogue between parliaments and the courts, Indigenous representative mechanisms create a formal framework for an ongoing dialogue between Indigenous peoples and the state. Indigenous peoples are constitutionally incorporated into the governing framework as participating political and constitutional entities, rather than primarily as litigants. Many comparable Western nations have bills of rights as well as forms of indigenous representation.

TREATIES AND AGREEMENTS

Treaties between Indigenous peoples and settler governments are commonplace in most of the former colonies, except for Australia. New Zealand has the

Treaty of Waitangi and Canada and the United States have treaties with Indigenous peoples. The treaties can be constitutionally recognised, as in Canada, or they can be outside the formal legal framework unless specifically legislatively incorporated, as in New Zealand. Treaties or agreements set out the key principles of the relationship between the settler government and the indigenous peoples, and can be seen as supplementing the existing constitutional framework, helping to set the parameters for fair engagement between the indigenous peoples and the state. Like mechanisms for indigenous representation, treaties and agreements tend to create a dialogue between indigenous peoples and the settler state.

In Australia, there has been ongoing discussion about the best way to effect Indigenous constitutional recognition in our nation, within our own unique historical, constitutional and political circumstances. Australia's Constitution is probably the hardest to change in the world. This is something that must be taken into account when considering options for constitutional reform. Similarly, there is longstanding resistance to bills of rights in Australia. Our nation's peculiar attachment to parliamentary supremacy means that we must be open to alternative forms of Indigenous recognition and accommodation.

Meaningful recognition will likely be effected through one or a combination of these three mechanisms—rights, representation and treaties/agreements—described above, through a combination of constitutional, institutional or legislative reforms.

RESPONSES TO THE EXPERT PANEL

In 2011, the Expert Panel on Constitutional Recognition of Aboriginal and Torres Strait Islander Peoples grappled with the need to recognise the Indigenous heritage of Australia while also removing the discriminatory elements from the Constitution and ensuring that no Australian is subject to racial discrimination.

The first issue relates to the existential crisis that Indigenous peoples face and that Australia as a nation faces. Properly understood, it is a crisis that belongs to Australia as a nation. The cultural and linguistic survival of Australia's first nations remains perilous, but it is equally true that the cultural heritage *of Australia* is in peril. The Indigenous heritage of Australia is the rightful heritage of all Australians—just as the British heritage is the heritage of all Australians. The Constitution is embedded with British heritage: the institutions and legal and political traditions it sets in place guarantee that Australia's British inheritance will live on in our land, for the benefit of all Australians of every ethnicity. The Indigenous heritage, however, is given little formal expression in our national and civic life. It is not readily considered the national inheritance of all Australians. How the nation might rectify this imbalance, and where the appropriate recognition of Indigenous heritage might sit, is part of the challenge of constitutional recognition.

In 2012, the Expert Panel recommended a constitutional clause recognising the Indigenous Australian languages as the original Australian languages, alongside recognition of English as a national language. It also recommended the adoption of a racial non-discrimination clause to ensure that no Australian is subject to racially discriminatory laws and policies. These two recommendations turned out to be controversial.

I was surprised at the negative reaction to the idea of a constitutional clause recognising Indigenous Australian languages and English as a national language, for which I was a strong proponent. Other nations like Canada, South Africa and India provide for constitutional recognition of their diverse Indigenous and other languages. Norway, Sweden, Finland and New Zealand officially recognise their Indigenous languages in legislation. Even in the United Kingdom, regional languages such as Gaelic, Irish, Scots, Welsh and Cornish are officially recognised as regional languages.

Even more troubling was the reaction to the Expert Panel's proposed racial non-discrimination clause, for which I was also a chief advocate. Despite the public polling that indicated a racial non-discrimination clause was the most popular proposal with Australians across the political spectrum, many on the right side of politics called it a 'one clause bill of rights' that would improperly empower the judiciary to strike down parliament's laws, thus undermining parliamentary supremacy. Of course, it is easy to argue that parliament should retain its unfettered power to racially discriminate, without judicial checks and balances, when you have never been and probably never will be subject to racially discriminatory laws. Indigenous people understandably have less faith that majoritarian parliaments will look out for their minority interests—history has too often proven otherwise.

AN ALTERNATIVE SOLUTION?

In search of an alternative solution to the racial discrimination problem, I endeavoured to engage with those on the right who most vehemently opposed the so-called 'one clause bill of rights'. These good-hearted, pragmatic, constitutional conservatives and empathetic liberals were not opposed to Indigenous recognition per se, but were genuinely concerned about the interpretational creativity of activist judges—a concern I did not share. I urged the good-hearted conservatives and liberals to help find an alternative solution to the racial discrimination problem—one that did not transfer power to the High Court or undermine parliamentary supremacy. They tackled the task with intellectual rigour and a noticeable lack of prejudice, and indeed the collaboration yielded an attractive alternative proposition.

The alternative proposition was that, perhaps, instead of empowering the High Court to decide what is in Indigenous interests, the Constitution could be amended to create a non-justiciable guarantee that Indigenous people themselves get a say in the laws and policies made about them. Non-binding advice, no expensive and prolonged litigation, no risk of laws being struck down, no High Court interference whatsoever. But the amendment could provide a constitutional guarantee of Indigenous participation and consultation in the political processes with respect to Indigenous affairs, creating an ongoing dialogue between Indigenous peoples and the parliament, rather than the courts and the parliament.

Parliament would retain a free hand to constitute the Indigenous representative mechanism. But perhaps the structure could be legislatively designed to give voice to those first nations who most lacked one: the Yolngu people, the Yorta Yorta people, the Wik people and so on. While constitutionally modest, such a reform could provide the impetus for a profound paradigmatic shift in the relationship between Indigenous peoples and the state and how the relationship is conducted in the political arena.

I warmed to the idea that the symbolic statements of recognition could then be effected through a declaration, outside the Constitution, free from uncertain constitutional interpretation—and in a much richer way than a minimalistic constitutional preamble could allow. The declaration could contain the statements of history and aspirations for the future. Perhaps it could be incorporated into a statute of reconciliation to set in place agreed high-level principles that should govern the ongoing relationship between Indigenous peoples and government. The statute could perhaps be enacted with the concurrence of all the parliaments, and with the active agreement of Indigenous peoples, to reset shared objectives and fairer terms for future engagement. The modest constitutional amendment could thus be supplemented and enhanced by fulsome forms of recognition in legislation, creating a compelling and political achievable package of reforms for Indigenous constitutional recognition.

CONTENDING WITH FURTHER OBJECTIONS

There are, however, further objections yet to be answered. While the good-hearted and empathetic conservatives and liberals could be brought around by the alternative proposition described above, there are still the objections of the more hard-hearted, unempathetic liberals who oppose any form of Indigenous rights or recognition whatsoever. This group argue that any form of Indigenous recognition would be unacceptable special treatment. They call the proposed Indigenous representative mechanism a 'race-based parliament'. Andrew Bolt is one such media commentator. The nation's leading liberal think-tank, the Institute of Public Affairs (IPA), is another. The IPA are attempting a hardline liberal argument against any form of Indigenous recognition. Their arguments, however, are susceptible to criticisms of internal inconsistency and hypocrisy.

For Indigenous peoples, a history of racially discriminatory and illiberal laws and policies under the Constitution prompts calls for constitutional guarantees of equality and protections of Indigenous rights and freedoms. By contrast, the IPA quotes King while condemning any measures for Indigenous constitutional recognition as inherently racist and contrary to liberal democratic values and equality before the law. Puzzlingly, however, a recent IPA campaign booklet, 'Race Has No Place: A Positive Case for Equality in the Australian Constitution', also rejects the proposal for a racial non-discrimination protection to entrench the equality ideal. [3] Many Australians would be understandably baffled reading the pamphlet.

This juxtaposition is not uncommon among the unempathetic liberal crowd. In his opinion piece 'Constitutional Change Will Divide, Not Unite, the Nation', Greg Sheridan on the one hand extols the democratic achievement of the equal protection clause in the American Constitution (the constitutional clause to which King famously appealed in the 'I have a dream' speech, which the IPA quote approvingly), yet on the other hand he rejects the Expert Panel's proposed racial non-discrimination clause as an 'anti-democratic' proposal. [4] When it comes to a racial non-discrimination clause for Australia, the unempathetic liberal turns suspiciously constitutionally conservative—they too become worried about activist judges. Why then, one might wonder, do they congratulate the achievement of an equality clause in the US Constitution and quote King with admiration?

Most disconcerting, however, for an Indigenous person reading the IPA booklet, is the justifying denialism with respect to Australia's history and Constitution. The IPA, for example, state that the Australian Constitution 'is based on the idea of the equality of all Australians'. Even on a basic understanding the statement is incorrect—it stands in direct contradiction to the IPA's own recommendation, in the same booklet, that the existing sections 25 and 51(xxvi) be removed from the Constitution because they are 'discriminatory' and 'illiberal' and give the Commonwealth 'the power to divide Australians'. Given that Indigenous Australians have in fact been denied the vote (Indigenous people did not have the same voting rights as other Australians until the 1960s) and have in fact been subject to many illiberal and discriminatory laws, the claim that Australia's Constitution was based on equality is not only unsupported by the evidence—it is offensive.

A similarly circular denialism is evident in Sheridan's critique. 'There is no doubt that throughout Australian history Aborigines suffered terrible injustice,' he states initially. A few paragraphs later, however, Sheridan argues that 'Parliament does not make laws designed to hurt Aborigines', thus contending that no constitutional protection against discrimination is required. So what about that 'terrible injustice' then?

For Sheridan, the practical significance of the discriminatory sections 25 and 51(xxvi) is minimal. The race clauses are characterised as mere 'anachronisms' rather than evidence of actual injustice—they are unattractive and philosophically incongruent at worst, but they are bereft of lived experience. For Indigenous people, however, the race clauses are reminders of a lived past. They are reminders of real laws and policies to which Indigenous people have been subject and to which (absent any constitutional protection) they could still be subject. One wonders whether commentators like Sheridan and the IPA have turned their minds to the human aspect of their arguments.

This lack of human connection is also evident in the way the unempathetic liberal tends to gloss over the constitutional complexities at play. They argue, for example, that the race power should not be replaced in any way to enable the continuation of laws that give effect to Indigenous rights, native title and so on. Yet the reality is that this would create legal uncertainty and risk such legislation being struck down, which might mean that Indigenous people lose what little legislative protection of their rights they have.

The IPA's ideological argument is deeply disconnected from any practical understanding of the Indigenous lives and communities the striking down of such laws would affect. And yet, as a liberal think-tank, property rights should be of great concern to the IPA. An Indigenous reader might well conclude that Indigenous property rights are not the same cause for concern for the unempathetic liberal as non-Indigenous property rights.

The IPA also glosses over the fact that simple removal of the race clauses does not fix the problem that is of practical concern to Indigenous people. It is not only the race power that is the issue. The Commonwealth can use its other powers to discriminate. The Northern Territory Intervention, for example, which many felt was discriminatory, was enacted under section 122, the territories power, not the race power. That is why some broader protection against the enactment of discriminatory laws is sought. Yet the IPA, a think-tank ostensibly committed to freedom and equality, has missed this crucial point.

Liberals should be the greatest supporters of Indigenous rights and freedoms. It is disappointing, then, that the most strident and outspoken of them are often not. Or perhaps this is unfair to liberals. I am increasingly uncertain whether the positions of the IPA, Bolt, Sheridan and others can be characterised as liberal at all. It would seem unlikely that a true liberal would automatically and without self-reflection view Indigenous rights and freedoms as less worthy of concern than non-Indigenous rights and freedoms. That, of course, was the predominant view when the Constitution was established—we are still dealing with the legacy of those views. It would be extraordinary if, in 2016, that had not changed. Yet how else can the inconsistency be explained?

Indigenous people might be puzzled, for example, that many IPA advocates and other liberals fulsomely support recognition of gay marriage, but they do not support recognition of Indigenous peoples. Why is it that these commentators argue for gay equality before the law, but they will not support the equality before the law guarantee that Indigenous people seek? If the discrimination present in the Marriage Act provides impetus for passionate liberal advocacy, then why doesn't the suspension of the Racial Discrimination Act in relation to Indigenous people—to be clear, it gets suspended so that government can discriminate against Indigenous people—prompt the same? Is it just about human empathy and lived experience?

It is probably reasonable to consider that institutions like the IPA employ and work with gay people, and thus may find it easier to empathise with them and the discriminations they suffer as human beings because they are friends and colleagues. Perhaps it is a simple lack of connection and experience with Indigenous people that causes the resultant lack of empathy for the denial of Indigenous freedom and equality. And yet, shouldn't a true liberal care about the freedoms of *all people?* It is hard to believe that the freedom lovers are such a close-knit clique that it is only privileged, white and gay freedoms that matter.

The laws that prevented Indigenous people from marrying who they chose, living where they chose, denying Indigenous property rights, preventing them from voting, and preventing them from earning equal wages—all of which have been allowed and unchallengeable under the Constitution (which is why Indigenous people seek constitutional reform)—in truth should prompt extensive liberal advocacy for change. The fact that the Racial Discrimination Act has been suspended three times in recent decades, each time in relation to Indigenous people, should be a cause of liberal outrage. Strangely, however, such denials of Indigenous freedom and equality tend to barely factor on the unempathetic liberal's freedom radar.

An outside observer, if they didn't know better, might be forgiven for interpreting such hypocrisy and double standards as simple racism. I would have thought things were not so simple, but perhaps in this case the simplest explanation is the correct one.

I hope, however, that the nation as a whole will be less hypocritical, more intellectually honest and more empathetic to Indigenous concerns than these unempathetic liberals would have it.

COMPLETING THE COMMONWEALTH

Our nation is in three parts. There is its ancient and original heritage, which is written into the landscape and ebbs in the veins of our rivers and seas. There is its British inheritance, the institutions and structures of government, transported from the United Kingdom to build itself anew upon the ancient soil. Then there is its multicultural achievement: successive waves of immigration bringing together the gifts of peoples and cultures from all over the world. These three parts entwine to form our united nation. They make Australia the unique country it is today.

Soon, if the political stars align, we will have the opportunity to formally bring together these three parts of our national story: our ancient Indigenous heritage, our proud British inheritance, and our multicultural triumph. Indigenous constitutional recognition provides an opportunity for a long-awaited reconciliation that could perfect our constitutional union, and make ours a more complete Commonwealth.

This could be, if we get it right, the nation's opportunity to finally include that which was historically omitted at Federation. Perhaps to give voice to those who have for so long gone unheard: the original owners of the land. It is an opportunity to put measures in place to ensure the wrongs of the past do not happen again. To protect the most fragile parts of ourselves—before it’s too late, lest we lose that which makes us unique in the world.

17

NAVIGATING A PATH TOWARDS MEANINGFUL CHANGE AND RECOGNITION

Patrick Dodson

Several attempts have been made to improve the relationship between Aboriginal and Torres Strait Islander peoples and the Australian nation state. Yet, despite these efforts, we have not resolved the deep historical grievances that linger from the unjust manner of Australia's settlement. While the disparity in our socio-economic circumstance is acknowledged, there has been very little effort to address the structural inequalities that have contributed to this. Nor has there been any genuine attempt to understand the differences that exist between us, or examine how they could be accommodated or viewed in an innovative or transformative light. The High Court decision in the *Mabo v Queensland (No 2)* (1992) 175 CLR 1 case offered the modern Australian nation state a unique opportunity to do just that, but the opportunity to reset the foundations of our relationship was missed.

In Mabo, the High Court of Australia rejected the notion of *terra nullius* but did not address the issue of settlement. The notion that Australia was unoccupied or *terra nullius* was used by the British to assert that Australia was peacefully settled rather than conquered or ceded, an assertion that enabled Aboriginal dispossession to occur lawfully in the absence of cession and treaty, and therefore without compensation. For many Aboriginal and Torres Strait Islander peoples, myself included, treaty- or agreement-making has long been the preferred option to recognise and fairly accommodate the unique sovereign position of Aboriginal and Torres Strait Islander peoples as the first peoples of Australia. A treaty could acknowledge the dispossession that occurred and establish a settlement process to redress and resolve historical grievances. It could also provide a framework to recognise our unique rights and cultures as Indigenous people and set out mutually agreed terms for our relationship with the Australian Government.

Constitutional recognition offers a different set of opportunities to that of treaty- or agreement-making. Although constitutional recognition cannot deal with historical injustices in the same manner as a treaty or settlement process could, it does have the potential to be reformative. Aside from acknowledging Aboriginal and Torres Strait Islander peoples' unique place in Australia, substantive constitutional reform could possibly take the form of amendments to prohibit governments from discriminating against Aboriginal and Torres Strait Islander peoples or create some form of Indigenous entity to advise parliament. It also offers an opportunity to remove racially discriminatory provisions from the Constitution.

There is concern among some Aboriginal and Torres Strait Islander people that constitutional recognition would diminish Indigenous sovereignty and make it difficult to achieve a treaty in the future. However, I believe that campaigns for treaty- or agreement-making are not negated by any of the current proposals for constitutional recognition. They are not mutually exclusive, and one does not necessarily cancel the other out. The Australian nation state could still enter into a treaty or settlement process with Aboriginal and Torres Strait Islander peoples if constitutional recognition occurred. What is required here is the political will to do so.

We cannot ignore the reality that the political will to enter into a treaty is distinctly lacking in Australia. Since Prime Minister Bob Hawke retreated from his commitment to a treaty in the 1980s at Barunga, no government, either Liberal or Labor, has signalled a willingness to pursue a treaty with Aboriginal people. The idea of treaty, like the notion of Aboriginal sovereignty, remains contentious in Australia, even though countries like New Zealand and Canada have had treaties in place for generations. Previous anxiety over the idea of a treaty arose from contested meanings of sovereignty and the question of who should the Australian nation state treat with.

Clearly no one single Aboriginal nation exercised sovereignty over the entire continent at the time of colonisation. There are, of course, many cultural groups or nations of Aboriginal people—each with different languages and affiliations to their own sovereign traditional lands. The diversity of Aboriginal people, though, does not preclude the possibility of domestic treaties or agreements (for example, a compact or a *Makarrata*—the Yolngu word meaning 'things are all right after a conflict') being negotiated and entered into with different Aboriginal and Torres Strait Islander groups/nations. Such agreements have the potential to provide a political framework for some form of local or regional autonomy and empowerment. The merits of such agreements, along with other options for treaty, should be explored further as part of a possible settlement process. Such a process, however, should not be conflated with the current process for constitutional recognition of Aboriginal and Torres Strait Islander peoples.

Constitutional recognition of Aboriginal and Torres Strait Islander peoples and treaty- or agreement-making are both important aspirations for the unfinished business of reconciliation. However, they are distinct matters and require separate processes. An amendment to the Constitution must occur within a prescribed process as set out in section 128 of the *Constitution Act 1901.* For a proposed constitutional amendment to be adopted, a referendum with a double majority—that is, a majority of 'Yes' votes in a majority of states—is required. On the other hand, negotiating a treaty or agreement with Aboriginal and Torres Strait Islander peoples is a political act that could be achieved legislatively. Whether an agreement power should be added to the Constitution for this purpose may also need to be considered.

Constitutional reform and a treaty or settlement process both require multi-partisan support, as well as the support of Aboriginal and Torres Strait Islander peoples and the wider Australian public. At the moment, treaty or settlement is not on the national agenda and we cannot assume that it will be anytime soon. Regardless, this should not deter Aboriginal and Torres Strait Islander peoples from continuing to advocate for a formal treaty or settlement process to be pursued.

What we do have before us is an opportunity to pursue constitutional reform. Currently, there is broad multi-partisan support for recognition of Aboriginal and Torres Strait Islander peoples in the Constitution. Polling has shown considerable public support for constitutional recognition of Aboriginal and Torres Strait Islander peoples; in the end, though, much will depend on the actual proposition. History shows us that Australians tend to be cautious when it comes to changing the Constitution, particularly if the proposition put to the voting public is not well understood. It is therefore crucial to get the proposition right and to reassure Australians that the proposition put to referendum has the support of Aboriginal and Torres Strait Islander peoples.

Constitutional reform is necessary for several reasons. Our Constitution makes no mention of the prior occupation of Aboriginal and Torres Strait Islander peoples of this country. When the *Constitution Act 1901* was first drafted, the only two express references made to Aboriginal people both related to our exclusion. Section 127 excluded Aboriginal people from being counted in the Commonwealth census and section 51(xxvi) prohibited the federal parliament from making laws for us. It was not until the 1967 referendum, when an overwhelming majority of Australians voted in favour of amending these two sections, that the scope of the Commonwealth's law-making powers was extended to include Aboriginal and Torres Strait Islander peoples.

Although the 1967 Referendum was a watershed moment, it did not deal with the legacy of racial thinking that influenced the drafting of the Australian Constitution. The concept of race therefore continues to inform the Constitution, with section 25 and section 51(xxvi) permitting discriminatory laws on the basis of race. If we do not change or remove these 'race provisions' from the Constitution while we have the opportunity to do so, we risk similar High Court determinations as we saw in the *Kartinyeri v Commonwealth of Australia* (1998) 195 CLR 337

(Hindmarsh Island Bridge) case. This case affirmed that section 51(xxvi) could also be used to pass laws that were detrimental as well as beneficial to Aboriginal and Torres Strait Islander peoples.

The Expert Panel on Constitutional Recognition of Aboriginal and Torres Strait Islander Peoples recommended section 51(xxvi) be removed and replaced with a new head of power, section 51A. This provision would enable the Commonwealth to pass laws for Aboriginal and Torres Strait Islander peoples, but in a manner that is not adversely discriminatory. It would also include a preambular statement of recognition, acknowledging our position as first peoples with continuing languages, cultures and connection to our lands and waters. A provision like this would not confer rights as such, but it could have the potential to frame how parliaments see and deal with us when they make laws that affect us as a people.

Consultations by the Expert Panel and the Joint Select Committee on Constitutional Recognition both indicated strong support by Aboriginal and Torres Strait Islander peoples and the broader public for some form of protection from racial discrimination. However, such a provision has proven contentious with constitutional conservatives, with some arguing such a protection goes beyond the intent of recognition and represents a one-step bill of rights clause. Unlike the United States we do not have a bill of rights in Australia and our Constitution makes few references to the rights and freedoms of the people. This partially accounts for the ambivalent response towards the Expert Panel's proposed section 116A, which has been interpreted as an unwelcome intrusion on parliamentary sovereignty. Governments do not like it when the validity of the laws they pass are challenged in the High Court, and any reform believed to shift power from elected politicians to unelected judges will likely face resistance.

Aboriginal and Torres Strait Islander peoples have little cause to trust governments and the democratic parliamentary process. The Northern Territory Intervention and the handling of the Mabo (No 2) and Wik judgements, in particular, confirm this. The primacy given to the concept of extinguishment in the *Native Title Act 1993* and its impact on Aboriginal tenure rights is probably the greatest act of ill will by parliament in recent years. Successive governments, both federal and state, have eroded rather than protected our rights in the period since. Recent debacles in the Indigenous affairs arena have brought into focus the dissonance between the rhetoric of 'recognition' and the disempowering effect of paternalistic, top-down policy. In their wake, Aboriginal and Torres Strait Islander communities are left pondering the merits of recognition as communities are threatened with closure, sacred sites legislation is watered down and vital community-based and community-driven programs are being defunded.

In the absence of a clear direction with respect to the constitutional alteration to be put to a referendum, it is difficult to spell out what recognition might mean in practice. Since the Expert Panel handed down its report in 2012, constitutional recognition of Aboriginal and Torres Strait Islander peoples has been left to drift for one reason or another. Despite two further reports deliberating on the process, we are still no closer to a decision on the proposition than when the Expert Panel embarked on this process in 2011. In the meantime, Aboriginal and Torres Strait Islander peoples have become disillusioned and disengaged from the process, and public awareness and support for constitutional change runs the risk of subsiding.

Strong support by Aboriginal and Torres Strait Islander peoples for the referendum proposal is absolutely essential. If Aboriginal and Torres Strait Islander peoples do not support the referendum proposal, there is little incentive to proceed to a referendum. That is why it is important to put in place a strategy to confirm Aboriginal and Torres Strait Islander peoples' support for any proposition before it is put to the voting public in a referendum—hence the idea of a series of Aboriginal and Torres Strait Islander conventions to be held around the country. The purpose of these conventions will be to discuss the various propositions at a local and/or regional level and appoint delegates to a national Aboriginal and Torres Strait Islander peoples' convention, where it is hoped a consensus view on any proposed proposition(s) can be arrived at.

The proposed conventions fall under the auspices of the recently established Referendum Council, which was set up to advise the prime minister and the leader of the opposition on how constitutional recognition could be best achieved. The Referendum Council acknowledges it is important for Aboriginal and Torres Strait Islander peoples to be given the opportunity to debate and clarify their preferences with respect to the matters proposed for constitutional recognition, a process that would in turn give clarity to the wider public about what Aboriginal and Torres Strait Islander peoples support in relation to the referendum proposition.

Lastly, constitutional recognition is not a foregone conclusion. We are trying to navigate constitutional reform within the confines of an inherently conservative institutional and political landscape, which brings its own particular challenges. While this means there is a need to be pragmatic about what can be achieved, it does not mean we need to settle for a minimalist or purely symbolic approach. So long as there is strong leadership and a shared commitment to achieve meaningful change that is legally sound and capable of being supported by Aboriginal and Torres Strait Islander peoples and a majority of Australians, there is reason to remain hopeful about the process and what we can achieve together as a country.

NOTES

INTRODUCTION

[1] Jill Stauffer, *Ethical Loneliness: The Injustice of Not Being Heard,* Columbia University Press, 2015.

[2] ibid.

1 FINDING A RESOLUTION TO CONSTITUTIONAL RECOGNITION OF INDIGENOUS AUSTRALIANS

[1] Megan Davis and George Williams, *Everything You Need to Know About the Referendum to Recognise Indigenous Australians,* NewSouth 2015

[2] George Williams, 'Race and the Australian Constitution', *Australian Parliamentary Review,* Autumn 2013, vol.28, no.1, pp.4–16, 6.

[3] 'Aborigines', extract from Second Reading Speech on Constitution Alteration (Repeal of Section 127) Bill, Attachment 'E', National Archives of Australia: A4940, C4257, p.155.

[4] Marcia Langton, 'Reading the Constitution Out Loud', *Meanjin,* vol.70, no.4, 2011.

[5] Brian Costar, 'Odious and Outmoded? Race and Section 25 of the Constitution', in John Chesterman and David Philips (eds), *Selective Democracy: Race, Gender and the Australian Vote,* Circa Books, 2003.

[6] ibid.

[7] Noel Pearson, 'A Rightful Place: Race, Recognition and a More Complete Commonwealth', *Quarterly Essay,* no.55, September 2014.

[8] In Patrick Macklem and Douglas Sanderson, *From Recognition to Reconciliation: Essays on the Constitutional Entrenchment of Aboriginal and Treaty Rights,* University of Toronto Press, 2016.

4 TELLING OUR STORY, OWNING OUR STORY, MAKING OURSTORY

[1] Nonie Sharp, *Stars of Tagai: The Torres Strait Islanders,* Aboriginal Studies Press, 1993.

[2] Sue Taffe, *Black and White Together: FCAATSI: The Federal Council for the Advancement of Aborigines and Torres Strait Islanders, 1958–1973,* University of Queensland Press, St Lucia, 2005.

7 SHIPS THAT PASS IN THE NIGHT

[1] Megan Davis and George Williams, *Everything You Need to Know about the Referendum to*

Recognise Indigenous Australians, NewSouth, 2015, p.48.

[2] Expert Mechanism on the Rights of Indigenous People, 'Indigenous Peoples and the Right to Participate in Decision-Making', Advice No.2, A/HRC/18/42 (2011).

[3] Native Title Social Justice Advisory Committee, *Recognition, Rights and Reform: A Report to Government on Native Title Social Justice Measures,* Aboriginal and Torres Strait Islander Commission, c.1995.

[4] ibid.

[5] ibid.

8 BUILDING A NEW, BETTER LEGACY

[1] Charles Perkins in a speech on Australia Day, 1984, quoted in Peter Read, *Charles Perkins: A Biography,* Penguin, Ringwood, revised edition, 2001.

[2] Bain Attwood and Andrew Markus, *The 1967 Referendum: Race, Power and the Australian Constitution,* Aboriginal Studies Press, 2007.

[3] Frank Lampard, *Reflections: 40 Years on from the 1967 Referendum,* Aboriginal Legal Rights Movement Inc., 2007.

14 IS THE CONSTITUTION A BETTER TOOL THAN SIMPLE LESIGLATION TO ADVANCE THE CAUSE OF AB ORIGINAL PEOPLES?

[1] Henry Reynolds, *Aboriginal Sovereignty,* Allen & Unwin, Sydney, 1996, p.178.

[2] Quoted in Michael Mansell, 'Constitutional Recognition Will Do Nothing for Aborigines', *Sydney Morning Herald,* 25 July 2014.

[3] Peter McAllister, 'Fight for the Right to Drink on Palm Island', *The Australian,* 4 March 2013.

15 KEEPING THE FIGHT ALIVE

[1] Riverbank Frank's 'The Message' reproduced with permission from the author.

[2] Megan Davis,' Treaty, Yeah?', *Alternative Law Journal,* vol.31, 2006, p.127.

[3] Native Title Social Justice Advisory Committee, *Recognition, Rights and Reform: A Report to Government on Native Title Social Justice Measures,* Aboriginal and Torres Strait Islander Commission, 1995.

[4] Teela Reid, 'Does Australia Need a Bill of Rights? Why, Why Not?', essay, Legal Theory JURD7223, University of New South Wales, 2014.

[5] Julian Burnside, 'Australians Must Challenge Unjust Laws', *Lawyers Weekly* (online), vol.3, February 2015, www.lawyersweekly.com.au/news/16115-julian-burnside-plans-to-stir-the-pot-at-alhr-annual-dinner.

[6] ibid.

[7] The Honorable Justice Margaret McMurdo AC, speech to the University of Queensland Justice and the Law, 9 October 2015, cited in Teela Reid, 'Does Australia Need a Bill of Rights?', op. cit., p.11.

[8] Gagelar J, cited in *Maloney v The Queen* (2013) 252 CLR 168, p.326.

[9] Teela Reid, ' Recognising Symbolism: Why a Republic is Part of the Resolution', *Indigenous Law Bulletin,* vol.8, 2015, p.15.

[10] ibid.

16 THERE'S NO SUCH THING AS MINIMAL RECOGNITION—THERE IS ONLY RECOGNITION

[1] Ta-Nehisi Coates, *Between the World and Me,* Spiegel & Grau, 2015.

[2] Martin Luther King Jr, Letter from Birmingham Jail, published as 'The Negro is Your Brother' in *The Atlantic,* 1963.

[3] The Institute of Public Affairs, *Race Has No Place: A Positive Case for Equality in the Australian Constitution,* Melbourne, September 2015.

[4] Greg Sheridan, 'Constitutional Change Will Divide Not Unite the Nation', *The Australian,* 20 September 2014.

ABOUT THE CONTRIBUTORS

Professor Marcia Langton holds the inaugural Chair of Australian Indigenous Studies at the University of Melbourne where she teaches and undertakes research in a number of fields, notably on agreements between Indigenous people and mining companies. She is the Chairman of Guma ICRG JV Pty Ltd, a Director of Indigenous Construction Resource Group Pty Ltd, and an advisor to the Empowered Communities. Langton has worked extensively in Aboriginal societies, especially in the Northern Territory, Kimberley and Cape York, contributing in particular to land and native title claims, as well as other community development projects. She has published extensively, including seminal works on Aboriginal film, video, art and artists, and has won awards for her writing. Langton served as the Senior Consultant to the major seven-part SBS television series *The First Australians,* and wrote substantial parts of the series book published by Melbourne University Press in December 2008. Langton's chapter in this volume is based on her Lowitja O'Donoghue Oration, 'Our Constitutional Reform Dilemma: To Win or to Delay?' The oration is an annual event of the Don Dunstan Foundation, University of Adelaide, and was held on 2 June 2015.

Harold Ludwick is a Bulgun Warra man whose traditional land lies west of Cooktown. He is currently the ranger supervisor on the Hopevale Congress

Biodiversity Project. Harold identifies with the 'Black Cockatoo' group from inland areas. He has spent many years in different communities in Cape York and has been advocating for Indigenous people since his late twenties. Harold's grandfather and grandmother are part of the Stolen Generations and this was the catalyst of Harold's push for Indigenous issues to be taken seriously. Harold is passionate about constitutional reform and Indigenous rights. Harold also represented Cape York in Geneva when presenting on 'Payment for Eco-System Services' on Cape York, a paper which was then presented at the Rio +20 Summit in South America.

Tony McAvoy SC is a Wiri man who was first admitted as a barrister of the Supreme Court of New South Wales in January 2000 and appointed as Senior Counsel in September 2015. He has a strong native title practice, having appeared for the claimants in numerous successful land claims. He also practises in the areas of administrative law, human rights and discrimination law, coronial inquests and criminal law. He was an Acting Part-Time Commissioner of the NSW Land and Environment Court between 2011 and 2013.

Josephine Bourne is a mainland Torres Strait Islander born in Townsville, Queensland. Her mother's ancestry is from Mabuiag Island and the Murray Islands and her father's ancestry is from Mabuiag Island and Moa Island. Ms Bourne was Co-Chair of the National Congress of Australia's First Peoples until July 2011 and was an inaugural director of the congress from its incorporation in April 2010. Ms Bourne also worked with the National Indigenous Representative Body Steering Committee. She has made a significant contribution to many local, regional, state and national agencies through program development and management, committees and working groups dealing with Indigenous education, community capacity building, multimedia development and youth leadership.

Eddie Cubillo is an Aboriginal man with strong family links in both urban and rural areas throughout the Northern Territory. His mother is of Larrakia/Wadjigan descent and his father is Central Arrente. In 2001 he obtained a Bachelor of Laws Degree and in 2002 he was admitted as a Barrister and Solicitor of the Supreme Court of the Northern Territory. As a Solicitor with the NT Legal Aid Commission he gained experience in most areas of general practice. He also gained invaluable experience working for the Northern Territory Government as a Solicitor in the areas of Commercial Law, Litigation, Aboriginal Lands, and Correctional Services of the Department of Justice. In 2002 he was elected to the ATSIC Yilli Rreung Regional Council, and subsequently became the Chair of that Council. Mr Cubillo has also been a former Chair of both the North Australian Aboriginal Justice Agency (NAAJA) and the Aboriginal Justice Advisory Committee (NT). Mr Cubillo has worked in various policy positions in the Northern Territory and South Australian governments. In 2009 Mr Cubillo completed a Masters of Laws (International Law and International Relations) at Flinders University. In 2010 Mr Cubillo was appointed the Anti-Discrimination Commissioner of the Northern Territory and following this, in October 2012, Mr Cubillo took on the role of Executive Officer with NATSILS.

Geoff Scott is a Wiradjuri man from Narromine in New South Wales with more than thirty years' experience working in Aboriginal affairs. Geoff has held senior executive positions, including CEO NSW Aboriginal Land Council, Director General NSW Department of Aboriginal Affairs and Deputy CEO Aboriginal and Torres Strait Islander Commission. Other achievements include appointments as Adjunct Professor at the University of Technology Sydney and former Chairman of the Australian Indigenous Leadership Centre. He was appointed Chief Executive Officer of the National Congress of Australia's First Peoples until June 2014.

Dr Megan Davis is a Professor of Law and an Acting Commissioner of the New South Wales Land and Environment Court. Professor Davis is a Fellow of the Australian Academy of Law and a member of the NSW Sentencing Council. Megan is a UN expert member of the United Nations Permanent Forum on Indigenous Peoples and holds portfolios, including Administration of Justice and Gender and Women, and is the focal point for UN Women and UN AIDS. Professor Davis's current research is on constitutional design and Indigenous peoples and an ARC project on the impact of extra-legal factors on the sentencing of Indigenous offenders of sexual abuse of Aboriginal women in the Northern Territory. In 2011, Megan was appointed to the Prime Minister's Expert Panel on the Recognition of Aboriginal and Torres Strait Islander Peoples in the Constitution and continues to be involved in legal discussions on the constitutional issues relating to the referendum model. She is the co-author with Professor George Williams of *Everything You Need to Know about the Referendum to Recognise Indigenous Australians.*

Kirstie Parker, a Yuwallarai woman from northern New South Wales, commenced with the National Centre of Indigenous Excellence in October 2015. She was formerly a Co-Chair of the National Congress of Australia's First Peoples. She is also a Director of Reconciliation Australia. Kirstie has a long and distinguished career in Indigenous affairs and especially media. Among other roles, she was editor of the *Koori Mail* newspaper for seven years, the inaugural executive officer of the Australian Indigenous Leadership Centre (AILC) and Director of Public Affairs for ATSIC. Her work has been acknowledged by multiple awards, including an Australian Peacewoman Award in May 2015, a Human Rights Award (Media Category) in 2008, and being named in the *Australian Financial Review* and Westpac inaugural 100 Women of Influence Awards in 2012.

Dr Asmi Wood has been an academic advisor to the ANU College of Law since 2002 and holds a position in the College as Senior Lecturer. Asmi gained a Bachelor of Engineering/Science (BE) from the University of Melbourne and a Bachelor of Laws (LLB) with Honours from the Australian National University. He completed his PhD in 2011 and his doctoral thesis is titled 'The regulation of the use of force by non-State actors under international law'. He is also a practising barrister and solicitor in the ACT. Asmi Wood received the Vice Chancellor's Award for Teaching Excellence from the Australian National University in 2010 and the Neville Bonner Teaching Award in 2015. Before commencing work at the College, Asmi worked in private practice and in government, both in Australia and overseas.

Nolan Hunter is the CEO of the Kimberley Land Council (KLC) and the Chairman of the National Native Title Council. Nolan is a Bardi man with strong links to his people and culture across saltwater country in northern Western Australia. His expertise in traditional knowledge has been further advanced in his role as CEO of the KLC, which represents and brings together about twenty-five different Aboriginal tribal groups from across the region. Nolan is an active campaigner for Indigenous native title rights and management of country. His chapter in this book is based on an opinion piece first published in *The Guardian* in May 2015.

Dr Dawn Casey has worked in a number of key Australian Government roles, including a period in the Office of Prime Minister and Cabinet. Her career includes the establishment of the Council for Aboriginal Reconciliation, and initiation of the joint Commonwealth and state response to the Royal Commission into Aboriginal Deaths in Custody. During her time as Assistant Director General AusAID, Dr Casey's responsibilities included Multilateral Development Banks, the United Nations, the World Health Organization and other international programs. Dr Casey is currently an Adjunct Professor to the University of Queensland and Griffith University and serves on a number of boards and committees. Dr Casey is a former Director of the Museum of Applied Arts and Sciences (Powerhouse Museum). She was the Chief Executive Officer of the Western Australian Museum from 2005 to 2007 and Director of the National Museum of Australia from 1999 to 2003. Prior to this, she led the authority responsible for the construction and development of the museum, which was conceived as a Centenary of Federation project. She is also a former Chair of Indigenous Business Australia. Dr Casey was appointed Chairperson of the ILC in October 2011.

Nyunggai Warren Mundine is a businessman, political strategist and advocate for empowering the first nations of Australia to build businesses and sustainable economies. His life and career have been shaped by a personal commitment to community and economic development. He is the Chairman and Managing Director of Nyungga Black Group Pty Ltd and sits on a number of business advisory boards. Nyunggai Warren is also the Chairman of the Prime

Minister's Indigenous Advisory Council. Previously he was CEO of NTSCorp.

Nyunggai Warren has a more than 35-year career in the public, business, policy, arts and community sectors, during which he has served as chairman of several organisations including NAISDA College, Australian Indigenous Education Foundation and Australian Indigenous Chamber of Commerce. Nyunggai Warren is a former National President of the Australian Labor Party and Deputy Mayor and Councillor of Dubbo City Council. He has received numerous recognitions for his contribution and commitment to Australia including a Centenary Medal and Doctor of the University *(honoris causa)* from Southern Cross University.

Nyunggai Warren is a member of the Bundjalung First Nation of Australia and a descendant of the Gumbaynggirr and Yuin First Nations of Australia.

Sean Gordon is the CEO of Darkinjung Local Aboriginal Land Council (www.darkinjung.com.au) and Convenor of the Empowered Communities (www.empoweredcommunities.org.au) Leadership Group.

Michael Mansell is Trawlwoolway on his mother's side and Pinterrairer on his father's side, both from the north-east of Tasmania. Mansell qualified as a lawyer, and from the 1970s has been the outstanding leader of the Tasmanian Aborigines. Legal manager of the Tasmanian Aboriginal Centre, secretary of the Aboriginal Provisional Government, author of many articles, Mansell has devoted his life to his people, defending their rights in the courts, and pushing to change laws that adversely affect Aboriginal people. His advocacy has often struck a raw nerve with politicians and sections of the media, though others admire him for his courage and tenacity. In 1987 he was chosen as Aborigine of the Year.

Teela Reid is a Wiradjuri and Wailwan woman who grew up in Gilgandra, New South Wales. She has a proud history of civil and land rights advocacy through her grandfather and great-grandmother. In 2010, Teela was selected by the federal government as Australia's Youth Female Delegate to the United Nations Permanent Forum on Indigenous Issues, which inspired her to swap a career in teaching for law. Teela studied the Juris Doctor at the University of New South Wales, and was elected Vice-President (Social Justice) of the UNSW Law Society 2015. In 2016, Teela was appointed Tipstaff to the Honourable Justice Lucy McCallum of the Supreme Court of New South Wales.

Noel Pearson comes from the Guugu Yimidhirr community of Hope Vale on south-eastern Cape York Peninsula and is the primary architect of the Cape York Agenda. Noel is a history and law graduate from the University of Sydney. In 1990, Noel co-founded the Cape York Land Council. Three years later, following the Mabo decision of the High Court of Australia, he played a key part in negotiating the *Native Title Act 1993* with the federal government. Noel's goal is to enable Cape York's Indigenous people to have the capacity to choose the life they have reason to value by reinstating the rights of Aboriginal people to take responsibility for their lives. Noel is a sought-after speaker, influences public policy debate and government deliberations, and has dedicated his life to the cause of Indigenous empowerment.

Patrick Dodson is a Yawuru man from Broome in Western Australia. He has dedicated his life's work to being an advocate for constructive relationships between Indigenous and non-Indigenous people based on mutual respect, understanding and dialogue. He is a recipient of the international Sydney Peace Prize. Patrick has extensive experience in Aboriginal affairs, previously as Director of the Central and Kimberley Land Councils and as a Commissioner in the Royal Commission into Aboriginal Deaths in Custody. He also served as inaugural Chair of the Council for Aboriginal Reconciliation and as Co-Chair of the Expert Panel for Constitutional Recognition of Indigenous Australians. Patrick is a member of the ANU Council, Adjunct Professor at the Broome campus of the University of Notre Dame and director of the Yawuru native title company, Nyamba Buru Yawuru Ltd. In December 2015 he was appointed Co-Chair of the National Referendum Council.

ACKNOWLEDGEMENTS

This collection of essays would not have been possible without the contributions of all the Aboriginal and Torres Strait Islander authors. We thank each of them for contributing to this collection. It is no easy thing to make public ideas and thoughts and aspirations for our people. It has been a long time since such a collection was published. We asked each author to forget about political 'pragmatism' and the usual barriers associated with law reform and create a vision—imagine—how things could be better for our people. Finally the editors would like to acknowledge the hard work and dedication of Emma Rafferty to this publication. Emma is the editor of the *Indigenous Law Bulletin* published by the Indigenous Law Centre, Faculty of Law, UNSW, and took on the role of bringing the collection to publication not long after commencing at the ILC. Emma's excellence in editing skills and lengthy experience in the publishing industry served us well in dealing with authors, deadlines and not-always-compliant editors. This collection would not have been possible without her generosity and enthusiasm and attention to detail.

BACK COVER MATERIAL

Why should Indigenous people have a direct say in the decisions that affect their lives? Australia is one of the only liberal democracies still grappling with such a fundamental question.

The idea of constitutional recognition of Indigenous Australians has become a highly political and contentious issue. It is entangled in institutional processes that rarely allow the diversity of Indigenous opinion to be expressed.

With a referendum on the agenda, it is now urgent that Indigenous people have a direct say in the form of recognition that constitutional change might achieve.

It's Our Country: Indigenous Arguments for Meaningful Constitutional Recognition and Reform is a collection of essays by Aboriginal and Torres Strait Islander thinkers and leaders including Patrick Dodson, Noel Pearson, Dawn Casey, Nyunggai Warren Mundine and Mick Mansell. Each essay explores what recognition and constitutional reform might achieve—or not achieve—for Indigenous people.

Megan Davis is a Professor of Law and Director of the Indigenous Law Centre at the University of New South Wales.

Marcia Langton AM is Foundation Professor of Australian Indigenous Studies at the University of Melbourne.

Printed in Dunstable, United Kingdom

91335473R00174